✓89-288

The
ENEMIES of
LEADERSHIP

Lessons for Leaders In Education

By E. Grady Bogue

Chancellor, Louisiana State University
in Shreveport

A Publication of the Phi Delta Kappa Educational Foundation
Bloomington, Indiana

Cover design by Charmaine Dapena

Library of Congress Catalog Card Number 85-62197
ISBN 0-87367-431-6

Dedication

To the faculty and staff of
Louisiana State University in Shreveport,
who expect the best of their students
and give the best of themselves

Acknowledgments

Work on this monograph was made possible by a grant from the Exxon Foundation, and I am grateful for that support. The following friends and colleagues reviewed the manuscript and made constructive contributions to both style and substance:

Jerry Boone
Arthur Chickering
Harold Enarson
Cameron Fincher
Fred Harcleroad
Ruth Jass
Joseph Johnson

Anne King
Larry McGehee
Ann McLaurin
Arliss Roaden
Robert Saunders
William Troutt

What strengths are to be found in these pages I can assign to their good editorial reviews. The frailties remain my own. To Mrs. Sue Carroll and those who assisted her, I am deeply appreciative of their cheerful and competent assistance in typing and proofreading the manuscript. To my wife, Linda, and my children, who endured the busy pecking of my typewriter in both early and late hours, I am grateful for both support and patience.

Finally, I am indebted to Derek L. Burleson, editor of Special Publications at Phi Delta Kappa, for artistic and effective editorial support and a working relationship marked by candor and cheer, a relationship of high professional pleasure.

Contents

Preface

As I read through current literature on management, and college management in particular, it is difficult to avoid the unhappy opinions held of leadership in education institutions. In George Keller's *Academic Strategy* (1983), I am arrested by this statement in the preface:

> Alone among the major institutions in the United States, colleges and universities have steadfastly refused to appropriate the procedures of modern management even though other nations regard American management as one of the ingenious contributions to the new world of large organizations and rapid change.

Peter Drucker's recent book *The Changing World of the Executive* (1982) catches your attention with a chapter titled "The Professor as Featherbedder." The chapter opens with this verbal salvo:

> In their own self-interest, faculty members need radically new policy in three areas. They need an effective substitute for a self-defeating tenure policy. They need organized placement of the middle-aged, average professor in work and careers outside of academe. But, above all, faculty members need management — either self-imposed management or management by administrators.

In 1976, former University of Cincinnati president Warren Bennis was very much of the same mind when he wrote in *The Unconscious Conspiracy*:

> Unquestionably, universities are among the worst managed institutions in the country. Hospitals and some state and city administrations may be as bad; no business or industry except Penn Central can possibly be. One reason, incredibly enough, is that universities — which have studied everything from government to Persian mirrors and the number "7" — have never deeply studied their own administration.

Are schools, colleges, and universities really among the worst managed institutions in our society? Although the views of experts quoted above are strongly held and eloquently stated, opinion does not substitute for fact. These and other writers hold sharp opinions, but I have not seen any seri-

1

ous and sustained study on the effectiveness of management in education institutions compared to profit-sector management.

It is true that we could easily identify case-study illustrations to support the thesis that education managers are often ill-equipped for the special trust they hold. However, for every case study in management malpractice from education administration, I can retrieve a better one – intellectually and ethically – from private enterprise. There is little justification for intellectual arrogance in either public- or private-sector management and every good reason to believe that both sectors can improve. *It is to the improvement theme that I devote this book.*

Education institutions do not exist to be administered. They exist for ideas and inquiry. Both those who teach and those who learn can be impeded or encouraged by the quality of administrative leadership at every point, from department chairperson to chancellor.

What are the enemies of administrative leadership? Perhaps one is that administrative performance is not anchored in a sufficient knowledge base. It is difficult to account for the human costs of conceptual shallowness in education administration. But those costs are real enough to those who know the damage caused by administrative amateurs whose only tools are worn sermonettes and homely quotations. Each one who takes an administrative responsibility should discover that practice informs precept. There can be no serious traffic there, however, if our minds are empty before we begin and remain so afterward.

Among education administrators today there are too few philosophers and too many managerial mechanics – enamored of technique, hurried and harried, seldom asking questions of purpose and meaning. There are too few statesmen and too many mannequins clothed in the fashion of power and status, thinly veneered in social grace – but empty in mind, heart, and spirit.

Our faculties are rightly concerned with the unexamined transfer of management concepts from private-sector settings to education institutions. However, they should be equally concerned with those who assume administrative responsibility with only sermonettes, vignettes, and common sense to guide them. Common sense has never been an adequate guide to scholarship or practice in any field, nor is common sense alone adequate for effective leadership in education institutions.

It is true that there is no administrative theory sufficiently embracing to cover all contingencies of the practitioner. In this respect, administration is no different from practice in any professional field. However, there is a rich conceptual foundation on which administrators can draw to improve daily performance. We are shirking responsibility if we fail to take advantage of good ideas and concepts at our command. How we acquire those principles and concepts – through experience or formal study – is of less consequence than whether we apply them. Administrators who disdain good

2

ideas practice an unhappy form of intellectual arrogance, a regrettable posture for those holding climates of learning and curiosity in trust.

A limited technical mastery of managerial concepts may not be our greatest leadership shortcoming, however. It is possible for us to be masters of technique yet find our leadership potential diminished by dysfunctional value dispositions. Technique must always be subservient to purpose. What we know will always be guided by what we believe. Thus the values we carry across the threshold of our office doors each day are no trivial matter. In 20 years as a college administrator, I have seen more managerial malpractice flow from ill-considered value dispositions than from technical incompetence.

In what forum will we learn to revere the dignity and diversity of human personality and to affirm the power and potential of our own personality? What book will teach us to absorb the hostility of the ill-informed and the ill-mannered but distinguish that hostility from those who express their loyalty in honest dissent? What seminar will encourage us to let neither dissent nor defeat deny us the power of an optimistic spirit? What lesson will require us to probe the limits of our integrity in lonely moments of decision, to find the renewing power that comes to those who exhibit both the courage and the compassion to expect the best of themselves and their colleagues? Where is the examination that will test our inclination to daring rather than to imitation? What course will teach us that:

> We as often act our way into belief as we believe our way into action;
>
> Thoughtful dissent is an essential antidote to leadership arrogance;
>
> Tenacity and patience are essential in the management of change;
>
> Majority affirmation of a foolish view makes that view no less foolish;
>
> Goodness is often timid and criticism loud;
>
> Opinion, forcefully and frequently offered, encourages its acceptance as fact rather than just opinion.

The renowned scholar Rene Dubos has observed that "human institutions must be held together by cohesive forces of a spiritual nature." It is the spiritual character of leadership that I hope to engage in this book.

A terminology matter. I tend to use the terms leadership, management, and administration interchangeably in this book. There is a convention that administration is an activity a little less grand than management. There is a convention that both administration and management are caretaker duties centering on stewardship of policy and program already in place. In this

3

convention, leadership is a higher status activity — one involving an entrepreneurial spirit, the breaking of new ground, the forging of new visions and ideas. For my purpose, I find it simpler to use the three terms interchangeably. A leader is not someone who can afford to dream only. A manager or administrator is not, in my view, someone who only works with his head stuck in minutiae, unmindful of tomorrow. Leaders, managers, administrators — I see them all holding in trust the future of an organization, its purpose and mission, its record of performance, its reservoir of human resources.

This book centers, then, on the theme that leadership is an art form whose effectiveness is improved by the mastery of leadership and management research and by the display of personal integrity. In the academy and out, effective leadership builds on both technical and ethical foundations.

I do not aspire to neat or embracing theory, though the reader will find sufficient theoretical referents for serious and further pursuit. My style is personal and normative — building on convictions that flow from research, reflection, and experience. I intend the book to celebrate the sharp edge of conviction, the beauty and the power of different leadership personalities. Given the diversity of personality among leaders, what exactly do we mean when we say that leadership is effective or ineffective? I believe that this book provides an operational answer to that question.

E. Grady Bogue
Shreveport
January 1985

4

Chapter One

The Limits of Common Sense

Curiosity and the urge to solve problems are the hallmarks of our species.

— Carl Sagan
The Dragons of Eden

What quality endows some administrators with effectiveness and condemns others to acts of malpractice? What differentiates the administrator who creates a climate of dignity and optimism from the one who sows fear and depression? What makes the difference between the administrator who can lift our spirits and the one who causes us to shun adventure? What enables some administrators to lead their colleagues to self-reliance, independence, and integrity rather than dependence and duplicity? What quality of leadership makes us want to do our best each and every day? That quality is artistry.

Management is an art form because it is the orchestrator of talent. In a *Harvard Business Review* article, Henry Boettinger asks "Is Management Really an Art?"

> At every level of management, from shop to floor to boardroom, across the spectrum of our institutions, whether government, business, education, armed forces, or the church, we need a rediscovery of the value of the individual imagination and rekindling of that passion for humane purposes which is the authentic light of leadership. To manage is to lead, and to lead others requires that one enlist the emotions of others to share a vision of their own. If that is not an art, then nothing is. (p. 64)

David Lilienthal, founder of TVA and former chairman of the Atomic Energy Commission, suggests that "The art of management...is a high form of leadership, for it seeks to combine the act — the getting something done — with the meaning behind the act" (p. 17).

5

In *In Search of Excellence*, one of the more widely read contemporary treatments of management and leadership effectiveness, Peters and Waterman tell us that a totally rational view of management — one emphasizing the tools and techniques of management, one centering on measurement and analysis — is not the approach that marks the really effective and best-run companies in this nation. Convinced that effective management is a matter of both mind and heart, they suggest that "The problem in America is that our fascination with the tools of management obscures our apparent ignorance of the art" (p. xxiv).

Administration is an artistic activity because practicing administrators must integrate theories on different themes, such as decision making, organizational structure, authority, communication, and personality, and different theories on the same theme, such as motivation. It is an artistic activity because administrators must engage issues of both fact and feeling, which lie on the boundary between science and philosophy.

My advocacy of administration as an art implies no lack of regard for scientific knowledge. I cannot envision an artist working without a scientific foundation. Those who ignore the impressive base of scholarship in management and see administration only as some charismatic mix of intuition and forceful personality are destined to carry colleagues and students in harm's way. Their mistakes will not bleed; however, they eventually will manifest physical and emotional damage of deeper consequence.

When the artist is alive in an administrator, he will have music in his heart, poetry in his soul, ideas in his mind, and fire in his spirit! The artist administrator is a thinking, searching, daring personality — an inventive and imaginative force in the lives of those about him, disturbing some and inspiring others. The tools of the artist are ideas and ideals.

The Limits of Common Sense — Yesterday's Heresy

Many practicing managers try to live by common sense alone. In the days of wooden ships, imagine the conversation in learned circles when a future-oriented soul suggested that ships might be made of iron? Quick proof of his lack of common sense was demonstrated by merely tossing a piece of iron into a pool of water. Before the Michelson-Morely experiment at the closing years of the nineteenth century, it was common sense that electromagnetic waves could not travel through a vacuum. Today, we are not at all troubled when we turn on our radios and TVs, knowing that the radio waves will arrive according to our new common sense. Before the experiments at the Western Electric plant in Hawthorne, N.Y., in the early part of this century, it was common sense that increasing the lighting in an assembly room should improve worker productivity. Today, we are at home with a new common sense: that worker productivity is a function of complex factors related to both work context and content. Today's common sense is often yesterday's heresy.

The history of management theory tells us quickly about the limits of common sense. At the turn of the century, J. Frederick Taylor inaugurated what some would later call the "efficiency model of management." During that era, the energies of both scholars and practitioners centered on time-and-motion studies to make workers more efficient. They studied, for example, the size and shapes of shovels in order to make ditch diggers more efficient. Taylor's work was, of course, far more embracing; and we are indebted to his model of curiosity, always looking for a more effective approach.

Years later in the human relations model of management, Elton Mayo and others taught us that physical variables were not the only ones affecting worker productivity. As we turned the half-century mark, the systems model of management taught us how the computer and sophisticated statistical techniques such as linear programming and decision theory could lead to improved management practice. In recent years, the quality assurance model of management has led us to see how involvement of colleagues can contribute to improvement of both quality and productivity.

In the recent *Theory Z* (1981) William Ouchi purports to tell us how "American business can meet the Japanese challenge." However, *Theory Z* may be only a restating of earlier ideas from American scholars such as Argyris (1964), Likert (1961), and Drucker (1967).

I am told there is still a Flat Earth Society in Illinois. Most folks no longer subscribe to this idea, though it was a commanding commonsense view at one point in history. Common sense alone is a limiting and sometimes dangerous guide to practice in almost every field.

In the field of law, it hardly seems common sense that a prisoner could have any significant effect on legal philosophy. We had progressed nicely from trial by combat to trial by peers, but the poor of this nation still stood before the bar pleading guilty more often than the rich. It took a hand-written draft on a yellow-lined tablet from a Florida prisoner named Gideon to get the U.S. Supreme Court's attention that a public defender system was needed in this nation (Lewis 1964).

Common sense in the field of economics is failing us today as economists scratch their heads searching for a new theory to fit what is happening in our erratic national economy and topsy-turvy world economic conditions. Not all the regression equations, not all the econometric models, and not all the research economists have been able to steady our economic Humpty Dumpty. The catechism of John Maynard Keynes has failed, and a new wisdom has yet to emerge.

In psychology, the commonsense understandings of a few years ago are exploding before new findings. How the brain functions in its analytic and holistic modes, how the intellect and intuition work within the brain is a fascinating new field of research that makes earlier assumptions in psychology look primitive indeed. As Western psychology meets Eastern thought, the philosophic foundations of psychology are being thoroughly shaken (Ornstein 1972). Interestingly, this research has important implications for the practice of management. Why are some managers so smart and dumb at the same time? Henry Mintzberg has an answer in his *Harvard Business Review* article, "Planning on the Left Side and Managing on the Right" (1976).

My theme is that common sense alone is a limiting and inadequate guide to practice in the field of management. Let me turn now to a consideration of the cost when managers attempt to base their practice solely on common sense.

Administrative Style — The Amateur and the Artist

The costs of our conceptual shallowness in education administration are difficult to measure. But the costs are real enough to those who have known administrative amateurs whose tools are worn sermonettes, folksy quotations, and experiences that may have developed as many bad habits as good ones. The following vignettes reveal the lack of artistry in our work. These illustrations are spiced with a mix of fact and hyperbole, but they are realistic enough for us to recognize ourselves and our friends.

Imagine a college dean down on the floor with greenbar computer paper spread over his office carpet. Beside him is his pocket calculator, which he is using to check the computer center's run on his budget for the coming year. He reviews each salary to make sure the recommended raise has been added correctly and then goes over all the equipment and travel budgets as well. Not so bad? Now add an associate dean and two department chairmen down on the floor with him, and let the scene be at 9:00 p.m., and you get a good picture of the management myope.

The management myope is the academic administrator who can see clearly the operational details before him each day, who pays careful attention to his in-basket, but who has little or no idea about where his department, college, or institution is going, what it should be or is accomplishing. Making sure the secretaries are in the office at 8:00 a.m., checking the locks on building doors, checking inventories, and other administrative clucking are activities typical of the management myope.

What are the costs of this administrative style? What does it cost, for example, for the dean to play on the floor with his pocket calculator — on a job that either a computer or a clerk can do — while his college wanders aimlessly from year to year without any clear mission?

An administrator's responsibility is to see that goals are defined and communicated. Administrators need not personally set the goals for an institution, college, or department; but they must assume a prominent responsibility for goal setting and renewal and keep a vision of mission before their colleagues.

What are the benchmarks by which administrators measure progress and performance? For many, progress means growth. Bigger has always been better, from both an institutional and a personal point of view. The measures of achievement are to be found in the increase in size of budgets, staff, physical plant, and students. These increases make attractive graphs as filler for annual reports.

This growth-oriented administrator writes bold lines, but often on perishable bond. With his eyes on the growth curves, he is oblivious to the bricks beginning to crumble, the computer being replaced for the fourth time in six years, and a building named for a former president being torn down for a parking lot. This same administrator is the university president who, fearful that the decline in enrollments reflects unfavorably on him, implements an expensive new recruiting program that requires a bigger budget than is allocated to some academic departments. If the president, vice president, dean, and chairman all think that bigger is better, then they all operate with the same rules of the game. Students learning and the quiet pleasure that comes with mastery of new ideas or skills escape their attention as they struggle to maintain the positive slope of the growth curve.

To what extent do the attitudes and expectations of the administrator affect the behavior of those with whom he works? Any faculty member can attest to the idea that the attitudes and expectations of an administrator can enshrine mediocrity or promote excellence, smother every dissonant impulse or nurture creative dissent. Too many administrators are insensitive to the relationship between their style and the actions of those with whom they work. Some of these administrators are behavior prophets. Their daily actions build self-fulfilling prophecies.

The chairman of a department of psychology in a regional university holds rather modest assumptions about the decision-making ability and maturity of his faculty. This attitude leads him to approach most departmental decisions in a paternalistic and somewhat heroic fashion: "I have to make these hard decisions because the faculty won't." The faculty members, of course, soon come to assume that their participation is not wanted or welcome. The chairman takes the faculty's lack of interest as evidence of the accuracy of his assumptions.

To be fair, the readiness of faculties to participate in institutional governance is sometimes equivocal. It is frustrating to attend endless committee meetings in which trivia are fondled and important issues are either ignored or debated into oblivion. Frequently, however, faculties have no chance to mature because no one expects them to, or because the chairman does not provide a climate and an opportunity for them to do so. The department will be fortunate indeed if a few courageous faculty members force the chairman into reassessing his attitudes about shared governance.

What are the costs if administrators fail to recognize that their expectations affect the behavior of those with whom they work? Most important, the growth of staff is inhibited. If a chairman or dean is an academic Simon Legree, the faculty will take fewer risks. Taking fewer risks results in less growth. Also, the faculty becomes more vulnerable to bad decisions because it is deprived of the growth experiences that come from the friction of involvement. The style of an administrator can permeate an entire institution. Some climates are so filled with tension and mistrust that they affect the physical and emotional health of colleagues. These costs are not recorded in accounts payable, but the price is high.

If an administrator's style has no flexibility, if it is unresponsive to variations in time, talent, or task, if with the predictability of the cuckoo clock, the same style pops out no matter what the decision stimulus is, then the administrator either is ignoring or is unfamiliar with a large body of management research indicating that the effective administrator is one who matches style with situation.

The "quick-draw" administrator may satisfy his staff when they go to him for a decision and get one on the spot. Such quick responses create an aura of administrative competence; but unfortunately, they may mark the amateur, not the artist. We admire the administrator who shoots the problem clear through with his first shot, who mows down those decision headaches with practiced ease. Sadly, the satisfaction of getting a quick decision is often shattered in the debris of ill-considered consequences. Why do we measure the decision-making ability of an administrator on speed rather than results? When action substitutes for accuracy, we should pause long enough to ask whether decisions made "from the hip" just appear good or really are good.

Some decisions on program, personnel, and policy do indeed call for administrative allegro; but others call for an andante deliberation. Deciding what color to paint walls in the lounge may permit a cavalier approach (even here it pays to pause), but decisions on increased workload for faculty should call for both deliberation and participation. The speed record of the "quick-draw" administrator should be compared to his record of decision successes.

Picture a cluttered desk and a cluttered calendar. In the eyes of some, such disorganization is a mark of creativity. However, the effective administrator knows how to organize resources, human and technical, to get the most effective match between task and talent. With the organization amateur, staff members are ill-used and become demoralized when their assignments and expectations are not clear. Simple processes are tangled up in multiple-part forms and repetitive checks. And in too many cases all communication emanates from the top of the hierarchy where the amateur resides. Obviously, an administrator should not indiscriminately impose an organization on an activity. Occasionally there is a temporary state of ambiguity before an organizational form will take shape, but a continued state of chaos is not productive. Organizing is an administrative art because it frees human talent.

At the registrar's office in a large metropolitan university are 120 clerks and 80 telephones, yet the most common complaint is that people cannot reach anyone on the phone. A look at the organization of the office is revealing. The work is so specialized that when one of the clerks is sick, is on vacation, or quits, the entire process falls apart. There are also too many layers of supervision brought on by a slavish adherence to civil service job codes. Nine supervisory levels separate the registrar from the lowest level clerk. In the records section, one clerk is responsible for the "A" records, one for the "B" records, and a supervisor is assigned to every two clerks. Each office supervisor has individualized memo paper. The office is an organizational nightmare, pierced by the ringing of unanswered telephones.

What are the costs, fiscal and human, from such organizational nightmares? Working with a few good conceptual tools, a new director of admissions and records reorganized both personnel and communications. What was the result? Within one year, the staff was reduced from 120 to 70 and a quarter of a million dollars was returned to the operating budget. This money could support a large academic program and hire a number of top-notch faculty members. How many millions of dollars are being drained away in academic support services each year because of organizational ignorance?

Administrative style is nowhere more evident than in the evaluation function. According to enlightened administrative practice, evaluation should be an ongoing activity, so much a part of everyday activity that it is hardly noticed. You discuss what you would like to achieve with your chairman, dean, or vice president. Presumably the evaluation of your performance is then based on that agenda. At promotion and salary review time, there are few surprises. Unfortunately this is not always the case. A faculty member or staff administrator may be the victim of a peculiar form of administrative immorality — evaluation based on a hidden agenda.

The dean of the school of business for a large university found himself out of favor with the institutional hierarchy but was at a loss as to the reason. It turned out that the vice president had expected him to concentrate on service programs to businesses, whereas he had been concentrating his energy on attracting additional research funds to support a new doctoral program. Somewhere in this misunderstanding the vice president failed to communicate his expectations to the dean and avoided dealing courageously with expectations and performance in an open and candid way. Another example is the newly appointed administrator who immediately makes summary evaluations of key personnel to decide who will stay and who will go during his regime. On-the-spot judgments based on the most surface and casual observations form the basis for decisions that can wreck the investment of years and throw an entire institution into trauma.

The newly appointed president of a large private university arrived on the scene in July and by early fall had dismissed three of his four vice presidents and two deans. Two or three months is not usually long enough to evaluate the competence of staff. In this case, however, the president became the victim of his own impatience and insensitivity. The speed of his action, the callous treatment of those who had given much to that university, and the ineffectiveness of those he appointed to succeed them were visible testimony to his poor judgment. Within the year he, too, learned what it was like to be fired.

Those faculty members and academic administrators who have been on the receiving end of such administrative style will bear witness to its human costs. To be evaluated on a set of performance expectations not known to you, to be evaluated in a summary way, and to be surprised by such evaluations at critical moments in a career — and often in the cowardly form of a memo — is not exactly a pleasant experience.

Other administrative styles can be seen in action around the halls of our schools and universities. You may know these styles: the *intimidation specialist* who is ready with critical questions and barbed remarks to cut down any and all ideas from his staff, the *sycophant collector* who gathers about him a staff that has neither the courage nor the competence to give him the truth about his institution, the *motivation expert* who thinks the major motivator of faculty is salary while failing to realize that recognition for good work and fresh challenges are reinforcers more powerful than any salary plan. There is also the *collegiate Cagney* who has the reputation of being tough but lacks the capacity to inspire others to action or thought; the *information wizard* who vacillates between character calibration and protective pussyfooting, between the desire to gather quantitative information on every phase of an operation and the conviction that nothing can or should be quantified. Then there is the *circuit rider* who moves every three years, knowing that the first year is a honeymoon, that in the second year his incompetence will be discovered, and that a third or perhaps fourth year will be required to find a humane way of getting him out of his position.

A Capacity for Wonder — "Turtles All the Way Down"

Effective administrative leadership depends as much on concept sense as common sense. If artistically tended, there are useful concepts to assist the administrator in improving effectiveness. Administrators are the organizers of time, talent, and task. More importantly, they are the organizers of ideas and ideals.

For a lighthearted illustration of the importance of organizing ideas, here is a vignette attributed to William James.

Following a lecture on the solar system, philosopher-psychologist William James was approached by a lady who suggested a theory superior to the one described by James.

"We don't live on a ball rotating around the sun," she said. "We live on a crust of earth on the back of a giant turtle."

Not wishing to demolish this absurd argument with the massive scientific evidence at his command, James decided to dissuade his opponent gently.

"If your theory is correct, madam, what does the turtle stand on?"

"You're a very clever man, Mr. James, and that's a good question, but I can answer that. The first turtle stands on the back of a second, far-larger turtle."

"But what does this second turtle stand on?" James asked politely.

The lady answered triumphantly. "It's no use, Mr. James, it's turtles all the way down!"

This lady had a perceptual vision with tight closure. Each of us with leadership responsibilities carries with us a vision as well. What we believe — our values — is quite as important as what we know — our knowledge. For example, I may "know" the essential features of Maslow's hierarchy of needs theory of motivation (1954), Festinger's cognitive dissonance theory of motivation (1957), and Herzberg's job content and job context theory of motivation (1966). But how do I take the concepts of these motivation theories and fashion them into a personal leadership philosophy of rewards and recognition? This is where the administrative leader becomes an artist, where he puts what he knows and what he believes in action for the improvement of practice and performance.

One more illustration: Almost 20 years ago, I became the registrar at Memphis State University, which in the mid-Sixties was in the process of growing from 5,000 students to 20,000 students. I knew nothing about the work of a registrar, but I was about to learn in a hurry.

At registration time I noticed that we had a lot of walk-in traffic. These late arrivals were getting rather rude treatment; they were hustled into a large room that served as a holding pen while we tried to figure out what could be done with them as we also carried on the regular registration. What did I know and what did I believe about this administrative challenge? I knew that Memphis State at the time was the only public institution of higher education in Memphis, a metropolitan community of over 500,000. I knew that the university provided the only higher education opportunity within reach of many folks in the community. I knew that it was the mission of Memphis State to serve the educational needs of that urban area. And I knew that our current admissions-registration system was ill-prepared to handle the walk-in traffic.

But what of the normative side? How did I feel? Should we simply turn them away, continue to treat them shabbily? Many members of the faculty and staff felt that it was unworthy of a true university to accept these late applicants, who had not disciplined themselves to meet the regular admission deadline. Their inclination was to establish an admission deadline and then adhere to it. Others held a different vision, and I was among those. My vision was that if these folks were eligible for admission, we should try to get them admitted and registered and to do so without disservice to students who had met the regular admission deadlines.

All of us new hires — the admissions officer, the computer center director, and I, all relatively inexperienced, naive, and not knowing that you could not do these things — put our heads together, and here is what happened. The admissions officer designed a quick provisional admissions process that admitted students contingent on their filing all admissions credentials within the month. The computer center director and I designed a supplementary registration system that let these applicants register on materials that were prepared for the computer (key punched at that time) after registration instead of during registration. Soon we had a system that could register walk-in traffic within 30 minutes to an hour after applicants presented themselves at the admissions office door. This was done without compromising our service to regular students, and it garnered considerable public relations advantage in the university community.

A simple illustration, perhaps. Consider, however, the rude treatment accorded students and faculty in administrative offices throughout the country simply because those who head them lack the service ethic. The only barrier to more effective service in this illustration was a normative one. Should the university adhere to an early and tightly controlled admission cutoff or attempt to serve the walk-in traffic? Which commitment most effectively recognized the university's role in the community at that time?

Faculties are rightly concerned about the unexamined transfer of managerial concepts and techniques from other settings to education institutions. They should be equally concerned about those who assume administrative roles believing there is nothing to be learned. Is there a more fundamental human business than learning? Lawyers are concerned with justice, physicians with disease and health, but learning is the fountainhead of both, and all else. How can administrators hope to inspire learning in others without setting a model of curiosity themselves?

The chapters to follow furnish more extensive and specific illustrations of the interaction between management ideas and ideals. As for this chap-

ter, my intent is to emphasize that the first enemy of leadership is ignorance. The effective leader is one with an active curiosity, a spirit of inquiry, a touch of irreverence, a compulsive use of that wonderful little word
"why." In a book now almost 40 years old, *Works of the Mind*, Robert Hutchins remarked that:

> The last question that will be raised about a prospective administrator
> is whether he has any ideas. If it appears that he has, he is unlikely
> to be appointed, for he will be rightly regarded as a dangerous man.
> (p. 150)

We need a few more such dangerous men and women, who have the first
mark of leadership — the capacity for wonder.

Ignorance is an enemy of leadership.

References

Argyris, Chris. *Integrating the Individual and the Organization*. New York: John Wiley & Sons, 1964.

Boettinger, Henry. "Is Management Really an Art?" *Harvard Business Review* 53 (January 1975): 54-64.

Drucker, Peter F. *The Effective Executive*. New York: Harper & Row, 1967.

Festinger, Leon. *Theory of Cognitive Dissonance*. Evanston, Ill.: Peterson and Company, 1957.

Herzberg, Frederick. *Work and the Nature of Man*. Cleveland, Ohio: World Publishing, 1966.

Hutchins, Robert. "The Administrator." In *Works of the Mind*, edited by Robert B. Heywood. Chicago: University of Chicago Press, 1947.

Lewis, Anthony. *Gideon's Trumpet*. New York: Random House, 1964.

Likert, Rensis. *New Patterns of Management*. New York: McGraw-Hill, 1961.

Lilienthal, David E. *Management: A Humanist Art*. New York: Carnegie Institute of Technology, Distributed by Columbia University Press, 1967.

Maslow, Abraham H. *Motivation and Personality*. New York: Harper & Row, 1954.

Mayo, Elton. *The Human Problems of an Industrial Civilization*. Boston: Harvard Graduate School of Business Administration, 1933.

Mintzberg, Henry. "Planning on the Left Side and Managing on the Right." *Harvard Business Review* 54 (November 1976): 49-58.

Ornstein, Robert E. *The Psychology of Consciousness*. New York: W.H. Freeman, 1972.

Ouchi, William. *Theory Z*. Reading, Mass.: Addison-Wesley, 1981.

Peters, Thomas J., and Waterman, Jr., Robert H. *In Search of Excellence*. New York: Harper & Row, 1982.

Sagan, Carl. *The Dragons of Eden*. New York: Random House, 1977.

Taylor, Frederick Winslow. *Scientific Management*. New York: Harper & Row, 1947.

Chapter Two

The Power of Leadership Philosophy

Life has taught me — and this is my luck — that active loving saves me from a morbid preoccupation with the shortcomings of society and the waywardness of men.

— Alan Paton
What I Have Learned

Just as the best medicine presumes health in the patient, better administrative theory must presume that natural rather than pathological processes are at work in most of the phenomena of university life.

— Donald Walker
The Effective Administrator

I have always been intrigued by the power latent in the expectations we hold for others. In early 1943 Harry Hopkins, President Roosevelt's closest confidant, was helping the President prepare his state of the union message. Targets for war production were to be part of the speech, and Hopkins cited a report from a panel of experts saying that the United States' economy, by straining every fiber, could produce 24,000 planes the next year. Roosevelt told Hopkins to double that number and add 12,000. The aircraft industry did not quite meet the Roosevelt expectation of 60,000 but did produce 49,000 planes, more than double what the experts predicted.

Most of us can personalize this anecdote. Most of us have had the experience of belonging to some group — athletic team, musical group, drama cast — whose energy was tapped by challenge of high performance expectations. And each of us can remember in our lives some teacher, some friend or colleague, who expected the best we could give. Prior to undertaking my graduate studies at Memphis State University, I thought a doctoral degree was something you needed to practice medicine. But under the caring guidance of a professor, my educational vision was elevated.

17

I persisted in my studies because I saw in the lives of a few good men and women high models of professional performance and personal integrity. And in those models was the expectation of higher performance for all whose lives they touched.

Of course, there is also the administrator whose style is empty of any inspirational quality, whose complete attention is commanded by dollars, digits, and documents. A friend of mine tells of an academic vice president whose concept of "strong administration" is being able to make the tough decisions. In a "shoot-from-the-hip" style, he mows down ideas from deans and directors and moves on to the next challenge. He is tough, but he lacks that inspirational quality that calls out the best in his deans and chairmen. The pervasiveness of his negative style dampens the spirit and enthusiasm of an entire faculty.

The German philosopher and poet Goethe said that "If we take people as they are, we make them worse. If we treat them as if they were what they ought to be, we help them become what they are capable of becoming." This philosophy has a practical validity for me. In May 1980, when my selection as chancellor of Louisiana State University in Shreveport was announced, a friend called me to offer congratulations and advice. He had learned that seven internal candidates at the university had vied for the position. After the usual words of congratulation, my friend asked whom I would take with me to Shreveport. I replied that I planned to take my wife, Linda, and the baby she was then expecting, and my Collie dog, Moses. I asked why he thought I would need to take someone with me. He said, "Well, Grady, weren't there seven folks on the campus applying for the job?" I indicated that this was so. He then said, "Grady, you are going to need a friend down there!"

But I thought not. I was going to Shreveport expecting the best from every man and woman there. If there was some departure from that expectation, I was prepared to deal with it at the moment of discovery. However, I would not dishonor the past record and the future potential of good men and women there by expecting less than the best of them.

Our attitudes, our values, construct our management realities. Believing is seeing! What can we find to commend this conviction on the power of our expectations? Here is a splendid opportunity to pursue the "ideas and ideals" interaction suggested in Chapter One.

The Philosophical Connection — Assumption and Action

Before exploring the research foundations on the relationship between expectation and performance, I want to engage in a bit of philosophical reflection. In our expectations we can enshrine mediocrity or promote excellence, tie down every Gulliver or free human potential. What differences in the behavior of our students would we predict if we expect success rather than failure? What differences in faculty performance do we elicit if we expect responsibility rather than apathy? And what record do we establish if we expect trust rather than deviousness? We may have the dubious pleasure of always being surprised if we consistently underestimate the potential of those with whom we work, but we can never know what the far limit of that potential might have been.

We need no flurry of footnotes to convince us that the administrative style of a leader can invade an entire institution. Roger Heyns, former American Council on Education president, put it well when he asked a class of ACE interns to consider the Watergate affair and "contemplate the pervasiveness of leadership. Every bit as important as pronouncements made, orders given, or policies stated are the leader's values, attitudes, and style" (p. 172). If a college president never takes a vacation, then it is more difficult for those who work with him to do so. If a dean is an academic Simon Legree, then it is easier for chairmen to get ulcers. And if a chairman is insecure, then there will be less risk taking on the part of faculty.

A former president of a large southern university made a regular practice of complimenting his staff in public addresses and remarks. If you were one of those who had done your work well, you could take pleasure in this mode of reinforcement. If you were one of those who had not, and you listened carefully, you could quickly discover what it was the president wished you to be doing better. This public expression of confidence and more subtle expression of expectation was a more artistic approach to motivation than a private chewing out.

Now some will say that this is Pollyanna foolishness. There are some folks who are just downright lazy. For them, you can't expect the best. Instead, get their attention by subjecting them to a good administrative temper tantrum; or as collegiate godfather make them an offer they can't refuse. Others will observe that this all sounds very much like Douglas McGregor's Theory Y management style, yet even McGregor had trouble being a college president on this theory.

The trouble with Theory Y, as with any theory, is recognizing the limitations of its applicability and therefore its effectiveness. Physical scientists are not necessarily upset because they have two or three theories to explain and predict the propagation of light, and they do not abuse the wave theory because it does not explain the photoelectric effect.

In 1969 I published a paper titled "The Context of Organizational Behavior." In the paper I suggested that:

> The essential theme of scholars in administration is that relationships encouraging dependence, submissiveness, conformity, and imposed evaluation must give way to relationships which hold promise for development of trust, for independence of action, for risk taking, for self-evaluation...

19

Yet the literature is equally clear on another point. It is that rigid and stereotyped notions of management styles belong, to borrow a phrase from Galbraith, in the museum of irrelevant ideas. There is no personality syndrome characteristic of all effective leaders nor a management style appropriate for all organizational situations. Flexibility is the key word. There is a time for independence and a time for control, a time for participation and a time for authority.

I have had 15 years to test what I wrote and believed in 1969, and I have found no experience that causes me to abandon what I said then.

This same theme continues to appear in the management literature. For example, in *Management of Organizational Behavior* Hersey and Blanchard ask "Is There a Best Style of Leadership?" (1969). They conclude that "based on the definition of leadership process as function of the leader, the followers, and other situational variables, the desire to have *a single ideal type of leader* behavior seems unrealistic" (p. 71). The same conclusion is reached by William Reddin in his book *Managerial Effectiveness* (1970) and by Tannenbaum and Schmidt in their 1973 *Harvard Business Review* article, "How to Choose a Leadership Pattern" (pp. 162-73). The effective administrator is one who can match style with situation.

Of all the books written on the college presidency and college administration in the last 10 or 15 years, I count *The Effective Administrator* by Donald Walker among the best. In a thoughtfully worded discussion titled simply "Trust," Walker suggests that one of the reasons we have trust problems in colleges and universities is our proclivity for motivational analysis (1979, p. 154). In a word, we have a tendency to assign self-serving motives to others and more noble motives to ourselves. Others are the scoundrels and we are the knights. We wear the white hat of the collegiate cowboy hero and those who oppose us wear the black hat of the villain. The administrator who begins to worry when he sees two vice presidents or deans engaged in hallway conversation has put on the white coat of the amateur psychiatrist.

In addition to the unflattering perception of colleagues cited above, there are two other problems with the motivational analysis approach to administration. Walker nicely captures both:

> Even were we all full-time, fully certified psychologists, psychiatrists, and psychoanalysts, we could not deal with people's motives or get inside their skins sufficiently to make motivational analysis the basis of administrative action. (p. 158)

> The problem with operating on the basis of motivational analysis is that too frequently other people's motives are seen as self-serving, Machiavellian, and expedient. When the actions of others are seen in this way, the human tendency is to respond with expedient and Machiavellian countermeasures. Everyone becomes locked in a circle of suspicion and hostility that has its own built in tactics and structure. (p. 157)

The managerial mind afflicted with this value posture has its own self-destruct built in. There is no way to exit the circle of mistrust and hostility.

We can find support for either optimistic or pessimistic positions regarding the power of expectations on human behavior. For example, in the disquieting little book, *The Human Prospect* by Robert Heilbroner (1974), he exposes some uncomfortable human inclinations:

> The explosion of violence in street crime, race riots, bombings, bizarre airplane hijackings, shocking assassinations has made a mockery of the television image of middle class gentility and brought home with terrible impact the recognition of a barbarism hidden behind the superficial amenities of life. (p. 15)

Heilbroner goes on to point out that the material achievements of our technology have failed to satisfy the basic longings of the human spirit:

> the values of an industrial civilization, which has for two centuries given us not only material advances but also a sense of elan and purpose, now seem to be losing their self-evident justification. (p. 15)

It is easy to find in the chronicles of the past sufficient reason for pessimism. But there is a persuasive counterposition. I find it nicely expressed in remarks by Rene Dubos, writing in the winter 1973-74 issue of *The American Scholar*.

> I believe that optimism is essential for action and constitutes the only attitude compatible with sanity. As the French historian Elie Halvey wrote to one of his friends in 1895, "Pessimism is nothing but a state of mind, whereas optimism is a system, the best and the most philosophical invention of the human mind." Optimism is a creative philosophical attitude, because it encourages taking advantage of personal and social crises for the development of novel and more sensible ways of life. (p. 16)

Here, I think, is the key. To argue that holding high expectations will elicit desired behavior is not to take an ostrich-like view that there is no meanness in the world, no distorted human personality. What it does suggest is that constructive and creative response to challenge is not likely to emerge from attitudes of defeatism and pessimism.

The record of higher education is not a museum filled with fossils of years gone by and finished works hanging on the walls. It is progress that requires us to address continuing challenge. In *The Ascent of Man* (1973) the late Jacob Bronowski reminds us that:

> man is the only one who is not locked into his environment. His imagination, his reason, his emotional subtlety and toughness make it possible for him not to accept the environment, but to change it. (p. 19)

We cannot place these human qualities in the service of education unless we first have the commitment to do so. The kind of optimism I have in mind is neither patient nor passive; it is aggressively looking for every possibility of constructive action within the realm of practical possibility. What can we find in the world of research to sustain our confidence in the proposition?

The Research Connection — Expectation and Performance

What I have shared thus far is personal experience buttressed by selected philosophical support. I place high value on learning from experience. In fact, experience may be the most frequent mode of learning for administrators. If good habits are formed by practice, the way to become a good administrator is to administer. But bad habits also are formed through practice; thus, bad administration is also developed through experience.

Fortunately, we do not always have to place our hand on the hot stove of experience to learn that we can get burned. As professionals, we also should attend to conceptual and objective data in order to put ideas in the service of improved performance. I now cite a few examples that offer some research support for my theme.

The first of these illustrations reveals how expectations can condition our approach to scholarship and theory building. I find it amusing but also disturbing. In *Principles of Behavior Modification* (1969), psychologist Albert Bandura reports a case in which behaviorists induced a bizarre broom-carrying behavior in an adult schizophrenic by periodic positive reinforcement. They then delivered the patient to a Freudian psychotherapist who was unaware of previous reinforcement activity.

In the case report, the psychotherapist wrote the following analysis: "Her constant and compulsive pacing, holding a broom in a manner she does, could be seen as a ritualistic procedure, a magical action. Her broom could then be: a child that gives her love and she gives in turn her devotion, a phallic symbol, the scepter of an omnipotent queen."

Now the analysis of this patient's behavior proceeds from a psychoanalytic theory base with a clear set of expectations, which are revealed in the case report. The analysis of the behavior is perhaps less troublesome than the therapy that might be prescribed. As a postscript, the broom-carrying behavior was easily extinguished by removal of the reinforcement and required no interpretive probing of the patient's sexual conflicts or repressed past. Those familiar with behavioral research can perhaps recall other examples in which the expectations of researchers have biased their findings. The lesson here for administration is that our assumptions do condition our perception of events around us.

The second example I take from a well-known study that dealt with the influence of expectations on student achievement. It was first reported in *Pygmalion in the Classroom* by Robert Rosenthal and then summarized in

22

the September 1973 issue of *Psychology Today*. Stay with me for a brief report of what Rosenthal found:

> Fode and I told a class of 12 students that one could produce a strain of intelligent rats by inbreeding them to increase their ability to run mazes quickly. To demonstrate, we gave each student five rats which had to learn to run to the darker of two arms of a T-maze. We told half of our student experimenters that they had the "maze bright," intelligent rats; we told the rest that they had the stupid rats. Naturally, there was no real difference among any of the animals.
>
> But they certainly differed in their performance. The rats believed to be bright improved daily in running the maze — they ran faster and more accurately — while the supposedly dull animals did poorly. The "dumb" rats refused to budge from the starting point 19 percent of the time, while the "smart" rats were recalcitrant only 11 percent of the time.
>
> Then we asked our students to rate the rats and to describe their own attitudes toward them. Those who believed they were working with intelligent animals liked them better and found them more pleasant. Such students said they felt more relaxed with the animals; they treated them more gently and were more enthusiastic about the experiment than the students who thought they had dull rats to work with. Curiously, the students with "bright" rats said that they handled them more but talked to them less. One wonders what students with "dull" rats were saying to those poor creatures. (p. 58)

I interrupt Rosenthal's narrative here to plead that we not dismiss the results thus far simply because we are dealing with rats. And I also caution against any transference of the animal label to colleagues of any variety. Let us hear what Rosenthal did next:

> If rats act smarter because their experimenters think they are smarter, we reasoned, perhaps the same phenomenon was at work in the classroom. So in the mid 1960's Lenore Jacobson and I launched what was to become a most controversial study: Intellectual Bloomers. We selected an elementary school in a lower-class neighborhood and gave all the children a nonverbal IQ test at the beginning of the school year. We disguised the test as one that would predict "intellectual blooming." There were 18 classrooms in the school, three at each of the six grader levels. The three rooms for each grade consisted of children with above average ability, average ability, and below average ability.
>
> After the test, we randomly chose 20% of the children in each room and labeled them "intellectual bloomers." We then gave each teacher the names of these children, who, we explained, could be expected to show remarkable gains during the coming year on the basis of their test scores. In fact, the differences between these experimental children and the control group was solely in the teacher's mind.
>
> Our IQ measure required no speaking, reading, or writing. One part of it, a picture vocabulary, did require a greater comprehension of English, so we call it the verbal subtest. The second part required less

ability to understand language but more ability to reason abstractly, so we call it the reasoning subtest.

We retested all the children eight months later. For the school as a whole, we found that the experimental children, those whose teacher had been led to expect "blooming," showed an excess in overall IQ gain of four points over the IQ gain of the control children. Their excess in gain was smaller in verbal ability, two points only, but substantially greater in reasoning, where they gained seven points more than the controls. Moreover, it made no difference whether the child was in a high ability or low ability classroom. The teachers' expectations benefited children at all levels. (p. 58)

The Pygmalion effect has been demonstrated in a variety of other settings — for bankers and insurance salesmen, for example. Readers interested in further confirmation of the "Pygmalion" finding are referred to a 1969 *Harvard Business Review* article, "Pygmalion in Management" by J. Sterling Livingston. For readers familiar with the Bible, the story of the 10 spies in Numbers, chapter 13, is equally instructive.

The third example I take from an article by Arthur W. Combs, "The Human Aspect of Administration" in the November 1970 issue of *Educational Leadership*. The basic question explored by Combs and his associates in their research was: "How can you tell the difference between good practitioners and poor ones in the helping professions: social work, teaching, psychiatry, clinical psychology, administration, counseling, nursing?" Here is what they found.

The difference found was not in the amount and kind of knowledge practitioners possessed but in their behavior patterns, especially in the quality and character of first or instantaneous reactions. Some important discriminating factors identified by Combs were:

1. Good helpers are concerned with people and poor helpers with things.

2. Good helpers believe that people are able instead of unable, dependable rather than undependable, worthy rather than unworthy.

3. Good helpers have positive self-concepts, whereas poor helpers see themselves as unwanted, unable, undignified, unacceptable.

4. Good helpers are likely to have purposes that are altruistic rather than narcissistic.

5. Good helpers are not concerned with what methods are used but whether methods fit. They are neither directive nor nondirective, hard nor easy, authoritarian nor participative.

I take interpretative liberty with Combs' conclusions to suggest that good helpers are professional artists who place ideas in action with a sensitivity to person and place. The second finding about the assumptions good helpers make of others deserves careful attention. In fact, there is a rich mine of concepts in all the findings. The one about the self-concept of good helpers finds support in Abraham Zaleznik's *The Human Dilemmas of Leadership* (1966):

> The exercise of leadership requires a strong sense of identity — knowing who one is and who one is not. The myth of the value of being an "all-around guy" is damaging to the striving of an individual to locate himself from within and then to place himself in relation to others. This active location and placement of oneself prevents the individual from being defined by others in uncongenial terms. It prevents him also from being buffeted around the sea of opinion he must live within. A sense of autonomy, separateness, or identity permits a freedom of action and thinking necessary for leadership. (p. 41)

The implication here is that the administrator who has the healthiest sense of personal identity, who knows both his strengths and limitations, will be the one from whom you can expect the most effective leadership. Test that idea in your own experience. We will visit this idea in more depth in Chapter Six.

Now, this closing illustration from the psychological literature, one sadly reminiscent of the Bandura example. To test the potentially damaging impact of "labeling" in mental illness, a study was conceived in which "sane" patients sought and achieved admission to different mental hospitals. The purpose of the study was to ascertain whether trained professionals could discriminate between the "sane" and the "insane" (Rosenhan 1973).

Once admitted to each hospital, the pseudo-patients tried to behave as normally as possible. The results: despite their public show of sanity, the pseudo-patients were never detected. Admitted, except in one case, with a diagnosis of schizophrenia, each was discharged with a diagnosis of schizophrenia "in remission." And how were the patients treated while in the hospital? Here are other disturbing results on the effect of labeling and expectations. One of the pseudo-patients approached a staff physician with this relatively "sane" question: "Pardon me, Dr. X, could you tell me when I am eligible for grounds privileges?" The doctor's response: "Good morning, Dave. How are you today?" The doctor then moves off without waiting for the patient's reply. The doctor, you see, has labeled the patient "insane." He expects no reasonable conversation from that patient and thus fails to perceive that the patient has asked a perfectly "sane" question.

Here the study becomes more interesting and disturbing. After being confronted with the results of this study, professional staff members — nurses, psychiatrists, physicians, psychologists — of a research and teaching hospital were told that during the next three months there was a likelihood that an incoming patient would be a pseudo-patient; that is, that the patient would be sane. Judgments were obtained for 193 patients, with these results:

Forty-one patients were rated with high confidence by at least one member of the staff to be pseudo-patients.

Twenty-three were considered to be a pseudo-patient by at least one psychiatrist.

Nineteen were considered to be a pseudo-patient by at least one psychiatrist and one other staff member.

The facts: actually, no pseudo-patient sought admission. These data speak forcefully to the power of our expectations and the damaging role of labeling. It is easier to label than to understand.

We do have evidence from both philosophy and research to support the proposition that positive expectations tend to elicit higher levels of performance. This does not mean that the administrator is always a nice guy, that he never gets mad, never raises his voice. But it does mean that by expecting the best from one's associates, one is more likely to get the best.

Before I close this discussion of the research support, there is another powerful motivational tool available to the administrator. This is the simple, but often overlooked, practice of reinforcing colleagues for work well done. The reinforcement of desired behavior has a research basis, albeit a philosophically controversial one, in the work of psychologist B.F. Skinner and others of behavioral inclination. We know from an array of research that proper reinforcement is an effective method of promoting the recurrence of desired behavior.

We spend a lot of time in our councils and cabinets talking about incentive systems, ranging from salaries to sabbaticals. While not depreciating the value of money and leave as rewards, it is surprising how much good effort we can elicit by the simple expedient of telling a colleague that he or she did a good job. It is equally surprising, and sadly so, how often this simple act is ignored.

I recently talked with a young research associate in an institutional research activity, seemingly a highly capable young professional. She indicated that in two years of work in that office, she had never received any feedback of any significance on the quality of work she was doing, or even on what she was doing. Here is a case where an administrator missed a good chance not only to elicit best performance but to develop a promising talent. On the other hand, I know an academic vice president who, with staff support, pays careful attention to the achievements of university faculty. By a personal note, a phone call, or in conversation, she expresses her appreciation of their achievement and accomplishment.

Recently, I attended a conference to explore the application of Personalized Systems of Instruction, or PSI as it is known. One of the major principles of PSI, as I understand it, is the use of immediate feedback to the student. This is a reinforcement concept and, of course, has its theoretical mooring in behaviorism.

Before the presenters had outlined the principles of PSI and explained the context in which it might be most effective, some faculty members attending the conference branded the method as fascist and authoritarian. One indicated that he "smelled a rat in the woodpile and the rat is B.F. Skinner." As I listened to those attacks, I wondered to myself how many of these same faculty members provided positive reinforcement to students and colleagues whose efforts were commendable. A word of "well done," carefully and sincerely applied, can do much to sustain good performance.

Intimidation Versus Inspiration — An Artistic Solution

The 11 February 1975 *Wall Street Journal* carried a full-page advertisement for a new book on business management titled *Winning Through Intimidation!* What the book offered was described as follows:

> It explains — in terms candid enough to make you wince at times — what intimidation is, why you become intimidated, and how you can avoid the mental lapses that occasionally cause even the most successful people to inadvertently, and unknowingly, become intimidated. And in doing so, it kicks the props out from under phony altruism and goody-two shoeism once and for all.

While offering counsel on the use of intimidation as an effective management tool and also on how not to be intimidated, there is no clue as to the possible outcome if two administrators have both read the same book. Perhaps there will be a sequel on "What to Do If You Have Been Intimidated."

Maybe there are times when intimidation is a useful management tool, but all that I have shared with you thus far clearly indicates that we need leadership by inspiration, not by intimidation. Is inspiration the "phony altruism" referred to in the ad? I think not. Someone has observed that "under carefully controlled conditions, organisms will behave as they damn well please." I prefer to believe, however, that the human spirit will respond to leadership by inspiration. Our students and faculties are the beneficiaries if we hold high expectations for both our performance and theirs, if we can find the strength to remain optimistic in the face of overwhelming problems.

Maintaining an optimistic attitude is not always easy. In some situations holding high expectations opens you to hurt and disappointment. But surely this is not a sufficient reason to expect less than the best. Others will say that holding high expectations is unrealistic considering what we know about human behavior. A decade ago the prominent sociologist Amitai Etzioni wrote.

> What is becoming increasingly apparent is that to solve social problems by changing people is more expensive and usually less productive than approaches that accept people as they are and seek to mend not them but the circumstances about them. (pp. 45-46)

27

He goes on to cite an impressive array of failures in attempts to change people's behavior. Such attempts include campaigns related to driver safety, drug abuse, and criminal behavior.

Etzioni suggests that our conventional approach is to change attitudes in hopes that changed behavior will follow. His message is that there are times when change may be affected more readily by changing the behavior and letting attitudes follow. There are sufficient examples in public policy for us to heed this counsel.

Indeed, Etzioni's article troubled me no little bit when I first began to reflect on what appeared to be his accurate reflections on human inclinations. Is this position hostile to the idea of expecting high performance from those with whom we work? Perhaps. But there is another way of looking at the matter, which may be only my rationalization. It occurs to me that, by holding high expectations for performance, we may be doing exactly what Etzioni suggests — helping to change the performance *environment*.

In illustration, this final reminiscence. Last year I had breakfast in the home of a former doctoral student, a man who now holds a responsible administrative position in higher education. I can remember first interviewing him for an assistantship. He was a student whose high school teachers took bets on whether he would finish high school. His academic record at the undergraduate level was far from spectacular; and in his master's work his grades were mostly Bs with a few As.

He had been teaching physics in one of the local high schools before thinking about doctoral work. I had word that he was a really fine teacher. I decided to take a risk; I gave him a couple of projects to carry out, a desk and a place to work, a little encouragement, and some breathing room. The results were phenomenal. I quickly learned that the only problem with his academic record was that no one had ever expected him to do much; he had never "turned on," so to speak.

I am not asking you to generalize from this one example, nor to accept uncritically anything that I have said. But I am asking that you review your own experience with leadership styles about you, and that you also consider the research evidence you can find, and then make up your mind how you want to approach the leadership responsibilities that may be yours.

In primitive medicine, evil spirits were considered the prime source of physical ailments and discomforts. That theory supported many a good shaman. In the course of medical history, the theory of evil spirits gave way to theory that movement of the body fluids was directly related to the development of disease. This fluids theory provided a rational basis for cupping and bleeding, and a thriving market for leeches. According to Norman Cousins (1979), France had to import 33 million leeches in 1827 because they had exhausted their domestic supply (pp. 44-46). More recent theories about the relationship of climate and disease led to the development of spas and springs. But modern scientific medicine has shown us that while spas and springs might soothe the body, for treatment of disease we must get rid of offending bacilli. Will radical mastectomies, lobotomies, tonsilectomies, and bypass surgery look as barbaric in a few years as leeching does today?

What of the leadership theory suggested in this chapter? In the future, will it appear as primitive as Taylor's efficiency theory now appears? Possibly. Meanwhile, in management as in medicine, we decide and we practice. An attitude of optimism and compassion seems eminently sensible, from both a philosophic and research perspective. Also, it would be well to keep our curiosity active, which, as suggested in the opening chapter, is the first mark of leadership. And it would be well to remember that:

> Expecting others to do their best is not the same as ensuring success, but it will increase the probability.

> Expecting others to give their best should not be used to make others the prisoners of our expectations but to free their potential.

> Expecting others to explore the far limits of their potential is not the same as making achievement sound easy. There must be real challenge to human effort and ingenuity associated with that expectation.

The act of leadership is to apply a touch of optimism, to hold high expectations of performance. Such an act may indeed make us vulnerable to betrayal and to failure. But it also opens us to the possibility of greater human achievement, to the satisfaction that comes in helping human potential unfold, and to the pleasure that comes when we call into action the noblest part of the human spirit.

Prejudice is an enemy of leadership.

References

Bandura, Albert. *Principles of Behavior Modification*. New York: Holt, Rinehart and Winston, 1969.

Bogue, E.G. "The Context of Organizational Behavior: A Conceptual Synthesis for the Educational Administrator." *Educational Administration Quarterly* (April 1969): 62-63.

Bronowski, J. *The Ascent of Man*. Boston: Little, Brown & Company, 1973.

Combs, Arthur W. "The Human Aspect of Administration." *Educational Leadership* (November 1970): p. 199.

Combs, Arthur W., and Snygg, Donald. *Individual Behavior*. New York: Harper & Row, 1959.

Cousins, Norman. *Anatomy of an Illness*. New York: W.W. Norton, 1979.

Dubos, Rene. "The Despairing Optimist." *The American Scholar* (Winter 1973-74): p. 16.

Etzioni, Amitai. "Human Beings Are Not Very Easy to Change After All." *Saturday Review*, 3 June 1972, pp. 45-47.

Heilbroner, Robert L. *An Inquiry into the Human Prospect*. New York: W.W. Norton, 1974.

Hersey, Paul, and Blanchard, Kenneth H. *Management of Organizational Behavior*. Englewood Cliffs, N.J.: Prentice-Hall, 1969. (See also the latest edition of this work published in 1982).

Heynes, Roger W. "Leadership Lessons from Watergate." *Educational Record* (Summer 1973): 172-74.

Livingston, J. Sterling. "Pygmalion in Management." *Harvard Business Review* (July-August 1969): pp. 81-89.

Paton, Alan. "The Challenge of Fear." In *What I Have Learned*. New York: Simon & Schuster, 1966.

Reddin, William J. *Managerial Effectiveness*. New York: McGraw-Hill, 1970.

Rosenhan, David L. "On Being Sane in Insane Places." *Science*, 19 January 1973, pp. 250-53.

Rosenthal, Robert. "The Pygmalion Effect Lives." *Psychology Today* (September 1973): 56-63.

Tannenbaum, Robert, and Schmidt, Warren H. "How to Choose a Leadership Pattern." *Harvard Business Review* (May-June 1973): 162-72.

Walker, Donald. *The Effective Administrator*. San Francisco: Jossey-Bass, 1979.

Zaleznik, Abraham. *Human Dilemmas of Leadership*. New York: Harper & Row, 1966.

Chapter Three

The Informing Power of Action

The picture is not thought out and determined beforehand, rather while it is being made it follows the mobility of thought. Finished, it changes further, according to the condition of him who looks at it.

— Pablo Picasso

We are producing the most educated, articulate, and brilliant sidewalk superintendents the world has ever seen. We have a limitless supply of people with intelligence and expertise to analyze society's problems, but very, very few with the motivation and stamina to leap in and help solve them.

— John Gardner,
No Easy Victories

It is always the same. I have something to write. A speech. This chapter. I confront my venerable Underwood typewriter and sit poised before the keys for uncomfortable and long moments. Playing hide and seek, the ideas I need lay hidden behind the closed doors in my mind. Then comes the rediscovery of a lovely principle. As I press the first key, the mental doors crack open and a parade of thought begins to march across the page. The very act of writing enlivens thought.

The benefit of linking thought and action is found in most every human endeavor. The doing of something — whether writing, teaching, banking, swimming, or leading — causes us to push our limits and inevitably brings us to fresher and more sensitive understandings.

Writing in their current best seller, *In Search of Excellence* (1982), Peters and Waterman describe "a bias for action" as one of those characteristics discriminating the high achieving company from others. They describe what they saw and felt in those companies: ad hoc groups busily at work on special projects, engineers and other specialists visiting in the labs of colleagues,

31

managers out from behind their desks talking to folks in hallways and shops. But above all there is the scenario of leaders willing to act in the face of uncertainty.

For the leader who is a slave to total rationality, the conventional notion is that first we know and believe, and then we act. We plan and then we implement. Quite as often, however, we may act our way into belief. Leaders who have purchased discretion and wisdom with their experience know this. And they know that action always informs and reshapes the original plan. Indeed, one may end seeking new goals that were not a part of the original plan, goals that emerged from the will to action.

This chapter tends to the proposition that there is an inventive and informing power in action, that one of the marks of the leader is an inclination to adventure. Doing, daring, deciding — these are the acts of the leader. The collegiate leader who has a will to action has made these discoveries:

That we are significantly alive in decision,
That latent powers are called to boldness,
That a will to risk is essential to achievement,
That the pain of failure may carry seeds of renewal,
That there is a payoff to persistence.

Let's examine these ideas.

Doing — The Informing Power of Action

Colleges and universities by their very nature are reflective organizations. In some instances, however, our penchant for analysis and criticism keeps us from adventures that might have informed us more deeply on the problem at hand. The ancient chronicles describe a debate of the scholastics. The issue concerned the number of teeth in the mouth of a horse. One of the younger monks, not yet fully socialized, was so bold as to suggest that perhaps a horse should be brought in and its teeth counted — an action orientation. For his impudence, however, he was smote hip and thigh and cast from the learned fellowship.

There is a certain warmth and security in the known. The risks of just thinking about a problem seem less painful than action on that problem. My purpose here is not to demean the power of thought and reflection. The pages of intellectual history are too potent for that posture. My purpose is to suggest that a reluctance to experience the discomfort of action without certainty denies us access to the discovery of how action informs and enriches thought.

When I was an aspiring AFROTC cadet in the late Fifties, I participated in a pre-flight training program prior to entering active duty with the Air Force. We were taught to fly a Cessna 172. I read the books. I knew what the stalling speed of the aircraft was. I knew what the aileron did. I knew what degree of flaps to use on different landing approaches. I knew Bernoulli's principle. But when my instructor jumped out of that Cessna 172 and I took it up in the air for my first solo flight, I not only knew, I understood!

A few years ago, two university friends were facing an outmoded registration system. They knew that a computer-based continuous registration system would solve many of the current system's defects. Between the dream and reality of that new system, however, lay a large uncharted territory. Anyone who has taken the responsibility to tinker with a university registration system knows that — with the possible exception of payroll — there are few administrative functions where mistakes will accumulate as much emotional steam from faculty, staff, and students. And under conditions of emotional overload, the steam often gets vented in the president's or chancellor's office.

These two — the director of admissions and records and the director of computing services — knew the validity of that old saying that you run faster when pursued. And so they created their own pursuit. They went before the university chancellor and his executive cabinet and proposed to plan and implement a computer-based, on-line registration system between the close of the fall registration and opening of the spring term. With yet another incentive from the chancellor (It had better work!), they set their minds and their staffs to the task. Problems that might have been whipped into an immobilizing lather under more reflective approaches yielded to the "can do" attitude of this team. Appreciating the merit of the goal, faculty and staff colleagues contributed ideas and energy. The very act of moving from idea to reality brought additional mental and physical forces into play.

In the fall of 1974, I left my position as assistant vice president for academic affairs at Memphis State University to take a one-year internship in academic administration with the American Council on Education. I chose to take that internship with the Tennessee Higher Education Commission (THEC), a state-level coordinating agency for higher education. Working under the direction of John Folger, then the executive director of THEC, my major internship assignment was to conceptualize a plan for allocating some portion of state dollars on a performance criterion rather than an enrollment criterion; that is, to have at least some state dollars flowing to state colleges and universities on the basis of an institution's educational effectiveness rather than its growth or size. Whether examined from a technical, philosophical, or political perspective, both faculty and administrators will appreciate the complexity of that assignment.

Keep in mind that all we had in the fall of 1974 was just the question: Is it feasible to allocate a portion of state funds on a performance criterion, to use state funds as a performance incentive? That feasibility question embraced both the philosophical (should we?) and the technical/political (can we?) elements of policy. Many colleagues across the state already had answers to both questions.

Nevertheless, we continued to push the question around the THEC staff for the better part of my internship year. We were able to get enough thought on the project to suggest a pilot approach to the policy question, one that would involve the voluntary participation of selected campuses in the state for testing one or two ideas, and to obtain some risk funding in the form of a grant from the Fund for the Improvement of Postsecondary Education (FIPSE).

A diversion here. The concept of pilot test for sensitive and complex policy issues is an important instrument for the action-oriented leader. Pilot tests are often relatively inexpensive ways to try ideas and practices in a minimum-risk setting. The pilot test is also a promising instrument to break in attitudes. It is sad to note how many policies are adopted full scale and fail with attendant loss of faith and money, when a smaller test version might have predicted the failure or produced enough wisdom and change so that a policy success emerged.

Now back to the main story. How could you place a performance incentive in the funding formula for the state's colleges and universities, an incentive that would perform fairly with community colleges, comprehensive universities, and larger research-oriented universities. A number of wild-eyed options were conceived — a state escrow account that would offer prizes for institutional performance, a Dow Jones Educational Performance Index. Eventually we reached the point where we felt we had sufficient educational and political acceptability to risk more public exposure. We set up a state advisory committee and a national advisory panel. And we attracted additional external funding support from the Kellogg Foundation, the Ford Foundation, and one Tennessee foundation.

I asked for an extension of my leave from Memphis State so that I might stay on and direct the funded project, and I employed William Troutt to assist me. Troutt was then an admissions counselor and representative at Union University. He is now president of Belmont College in Nashville. We brought our national advisory panel to Nashville in the fall of 1975 to review our plan of attack. They devastated the plan. I remember, as Troutt and I drove home that evening in his Ford Mustang, wondering whether we should consider an immediate return to our universities.

However, on Monday morning we buckled up and started over. The end of the story is told in Chapter Five, where the policy finally adopted in Tennessee is described. And the full story is told in the project report (Bogue 1980). The difficulty is that there is no document that adequately conveys the conceptual and emotional defeat we often felt, how those defeats first dampened our spirits and then sharpened our determination, how original ideas were discarded or sharply revised by our experience.

To see the end of every leadership journey is not always possible. The very act of the journey may carry one to newer and more exciting destinations, destinations that might not have been conceivable when one took the first step. Real world Hobbits, leaders who have the will to take the first step will find an excitement in the journey. The will to act assumes a will to dare.

Daring — The Rewards of Risk

I have never been much of a water enthusiast. I can swim, but my skinny legs and abundance of freckles have never made beaches and lakes fun places for me. I was almost 40 before I learned to water ski. When I considered the dubious support of the small life preserver wrapped loosely around my waist and the unknown depth of Lake Hamilton in Arkansas, the prospect of jumping from the boat was not exactly one of the grander moments in my life.

Nevertheless, over the side I went under the watchful and suspicious eyes of several companions. I fussed with the skis but was unable to get them affixed until a friend swam out and placed a second life jacket around me, one of those vest life jackets. The embarrassment of it all. The two life jackets not withstanding, I spent the next 30 minutes plowing around underneath Lake Hamilton.

After much coaching and yelling from companions in the boat, I finally popped out of the water and enjoyed the exhilaration of skimming across the top of the lake. This was a moment of daring in my life. After all, someone with my skinny legs should never get more than a few miles from home, much less put on water skis. What was a big moment for me would have been child's play for one who had been around the water since toddler years. Now once I discovered that you could stay on top of the water on those things, I had a great day. The pleasure of mastery came after, not before, the willingness to make the leap.

The love of security is an understandable and natural human inclination. Like our children, we don't like books that don't have answers in the back. We yearn for the warmth of the familiar and the guarantee of success.

This last year at Louisiana State University in Shreveport, we completed our 10-year accreditation self-study for the Southern Association of Colleges and Schools (SACS). As we began the self-study, we thought it might prove useful to use the experience as a stimulus to launch the university into a more effective evaluation cycle — giving a little more careful attention to unit and institutional goal definition, achievement recognition, and resource allocation.

When this idea was first mentioned to faculty and administrative leadership, some wanted to continue with the conventional standards of the college delegate assembly (SACS 1977). Review the standards, assemble the data tables, answer the questions, get the self-study completed, and be assured of educational salvation for another 10 years.

Perhaps it was arrogance on my part, but I was quite confident that the university would be recommended for accreditation by our peers. We could have met all the standards without breathing hard; we had some good educational performance data and a track record of fiscal management integrity, and all our program and enrollment trend data looked promising. Why not relax on the question of whether we would be accredited, I suggested, and use the self-study as an opportunity to push a little beyond the known, to create a sense of institutional pursuit, if you will. To the credit of our faculty and staff, a good sense of adventure did prevail; and we enjoyed the pleasure of learning about planning by planning.

Just that simple? Not at all. We had lively arguments on the difference between a "goal" and an "objective," on whether all the paper we were generating would make any differences in budgeting, on what the word "priority" meant, on who was responsible for planning, and on what all this meant for individual faculty members. But at least we now have the semblance of a planning system that had not existed before, and I'll be saying more about that in Chapter Four.

If these moments were not enough to liven up the accreditation process at our university, we were called in the middle of that self-study and asked by SACS staff if we might also be willing to pilot test a new set of *Criteria for Accreditation* (SACS 1982), which SACS was then getting ready to place before its membership. Again, a pleasant sense of adventure continued, and we agreed to this pilot test. The visit of the peer committee in the fall of 1983 was a productive exercise.

This story has a further dimension. When the new *Criteria for Accreditation* came up for review at the annual meeting of SACS in December 1983, the draft document emphasizing planning and student outcomes assessment was set aside for further study. There was high anxiety on the floor during the debate on these new criteria. To be sure, a part of that uncertainty and anxiety flowed from legitimate conceptual concerns over the wording and application of the *Criteria*. Whether the new *Criteria* had been adequately presented in a series of regional hearings across the South was another question. But a good portion of anxiety could be traced to certain ambiguity in the *Criteria*.

You see, the new *Criteria* are not written with as much closure as the old standards. Deliberately, the new criteria leave a good bit of discretion and independence to a campus in the definition of its goals and in the selection of effectiveness indicators appropriate to its own mission. To some institutional officers and faculty this uncertainty was seriously discomforting. They want to be told exactly what instruments are to be employed, what data are to be gathered, what results are to be expected, what standards of performance on outcomes are acceptable. The presence of ambiguity or openness in the new criteria did not provide that guarantee of educational salvation.

For those who believe in the merit of voluntary accreditation, this story has a happy postscript. In December 1984, the SACS fully adopted the revised *Criteria for Accreditation*. These criteria include a statement on "Planning and Evaluation."

To cause both ourselves and our institutions to live a little beyond our capacity is a difficult test of leadership, but essential to learning and renewal. Perhaps our reluctance to discover the renewing power of daring turns on our fear of failure. Let's direct our attention there for a moment and see whether we might find yet another leadership lesson.

Failing — Arrivals and Journeys

On my office wall hang two framed quotations, "The Art of Adventure" and "The Art of Failure," from Wilferd Peterson's *The Art of Living* (1961). They remind me that every adventure is always accompanied by the prospect of failure. I do not know many who enjoy defeat or failure in their lives. I don't. I want to manage and control so that I can avoid surprises, vulnerability, hurt, disappointment. Perhaps this fear of failure is what immobilizes leadership, keeps us from decision and daring.

I began this chapter with a personal note about learning to fly a Cessna 172 prior to active duty with the Air Force. On my way to the wild blue yonder, I encountered a detour. During my first week of active duty in San Antonio, I failed the flight physical. The Air Force eventually transferred me from my flight training assignment to electronics school at Keesler Air Force Base in Mississippi. In the interim I was assigned to take inventory in the base exchange at Lackland Air Force Base.

To the disappointment of failing out of flight training was added the ignominy of assignment to take inventory in the ladies-wear section of the base exchange. Here, a salty lady with 25 years of civil service experience managed to keep my face on red alert for three days. As she sorted articles of ladies wear, I tallied. Then after our coffee break, I counted and she tallied. After a day of this, I returned to the Bachelor's Officers Quarters and re-examined my commission from the President of the United States where I read that I was "to observe and follow such orders and directions from time to time, as may be given by the President or future Presidents." The next day I returned to my embarrassing assignment certain that as soon as the President learned that I had been ordered to count bras and panties, an assignment to more macho duty would soon be forthcoming.

How does one handle that disappointment? I saw young men whose spirit would not allow them to flex. Their hearts and minds had been set on flying. And when that door slammed shut, they could not find another open. A few went into depression. A few became cynical and bitter. A few

37

departed the Air Force. I went on to electronics school where my math and physics degree found fertile challenge, served three-and-a-half years, met men different from me, and learned a lot about myself, about others, about leadership.

Failure can hurt. But there is a flip side to failure that one can only discern when you get on the other side. In *The Shantung Compound* (1966), American theologian Langdon Gilkey has written a fascinating narrative of 2,000 men and women imprisoned by the Japanese in World War II. This imprisonment was an unanticipated event in the lives of these men and women. Representing a cross section of humanity, this forced mini-society of professors and prostitutes, missionaries and mothers, doctors and dandies had to fashion their own morality and rules for such basic decisions as the allocation of living space, food, and such responsibilities as cooking and policing. All this without the usual external sanctions we take for granted in an ordered society.

One could find no stoplights, courts, or policemen when this mini-society began. The torture these men and women faced was not physical torture but the moral torture of building a society with all the props taken away. Think about it. What concepts of morality and justice would emerge if we chose a random sample of 2,000 folks from any community and placed them in a camp without the usual sanctions of law and order?

But parlor discussion was of little value in the Shantung Compound! Gilkey came to the conclusion that moral health was as important as material supplies and services. As he watched and participated in the ethical and civil struggle of this mini-society, he concluded that the question of "what is right" is never far from the question of "what is possible." Physicians turned out to be political cowards, ministers were filled with holiness but empty of compassion. Those who engaged the political issues of that forced society became what all statesman politicians become — philosophers of the first order.

Here is one reminiscence rich in meaning and directly pertinent to the point at hand:

> One of the strangest lessons that our unstable life passage teaches us is that the unwanted is often creative rather than destructive. No one wished to go to Weihsien camp. Yet such an experience, resisted and abhorred, had within it the seeds of new insight and thus of new life for many of us. Almost because of its discomfort, its turmoil, and its boredom, it eventually became the source of certainties and of convictions with which life would henceforth be more creatively faced. This is a common mystery of life, an aspect, if you will, of common grace: out of apparent evil, new creativity can arise if the meanings and possibilities latent within the new situation are grasped with courage and with faith. (p. 242)

There are few men and women who wear the mantle of leader with any grace or competence who do not have pain lines etched in mind and heart, and often in body. As with Gilkey, life has intervened and pulled them from familiar paths, trusted relationships, and certain achievement; brought tears of anguish and pushed them to the edge of despair, even disbelief; accented their solitude and forced them to look at the personal and often frightening issue of meaning in their lives. Is it so hard, then, for us to understand what Gilkey is saying — that when we are pulled from the womb of certainty, our ability has opportunity for exercise, our pain enriches our capacity for compassion, our failure often forges a new strength. These are not matters often discussed in either management or leadership texts. You can find them manifest, however, in every page of biography.

Earlier in the chapter, I spoke of my leaving Memphis State University in the fall of 1974 to take a one-year internship with the Tennessee Higher Education Commission. At the time of my departure, the gentlemen's understanding with the president was that I might return at the conclusion of the internship to become dean of an Experimental College, the idea of which was then being incubated by a faculty committee I had been chairing. I encouraged then President Billy Mac Jones to use a national screening committee to satisfy affirmative action policy and to honor the rich base of faculty involvement thus far in that project. Was it naiveté, arrogance, or confidence? I believed that I could make the final five in that screening.

I didn't! I had not come the traditional route to university administration (if there is such a route), had not held a tenured faculty appointment. And further I was the kid who had grown up at Memphis State. I had all three of my degrees from there. These factors — and perhaps others as well — conspired against my candidacy. I will never know. And thus, in the spring of 1975 I faced the disappointment of having failed in that search, turned down by my home colleagues. Not one of the happier moments in my life.

About that time, however, came the opportunity to direct the Performance Funding project of the THEC, the project earlier described in this chapter. And thus in the late spring of 1975, I moved my attention from the disappointment at Memphis State to the new challenge in Nashville. And then fate intervened again. In mid-summer the academic officer of the commission resigned, which left a vacancy in that position. Wayne Brown, the newly appointed executive director of THEC, asked me to take that responsibility on an acting basis. A short while later, the commission and Brown asked that I take the appointment on a permanent basis. I ended up with a pleasant new professional challenge and with a salary higher than the one I would have received if I had returned to Memphis State as dean.

In both our scientific and social laboratories, it is sad that we too often teach our students only the arrival and not the journey. We teach them principles, theories, and convictions devoid of the pain, the anxiety, the doubt it took to produce them. Perhaps if we just had them read this lovely line from Gibran it might help: "One may not reach the dawn save by the path of night" (1973, p. 8). Daring, not infallibility, is the mark of leadership.

Persisting — The Fruits of Tenacity

A corollary of the will to action is persistence toward a goal. The values of bulldog tenacity are known to any leader. The word "persistence" and the phrase "bulldog tenacity" suggest successive charges in the same direction with the same tactics until barriers yield to the force and frequency of our attack. What I want to treat in this final section, however, is a leader option turning more on finesse than force. A mark of the leader is that he searches for alternative routes when conventional ones constrict. Another way to view the matter is that leaders look for leverage that yields an advantage. Consider the great defensive barriers of history — the Maginot Line, the Great Wall of China. Their impotence was due not so much to a breaching of the barriers as it was to the discovery of alternative routes to get behind these barriers.

Best-selling author Frederick Forsyth has written some fascinating short stories in a collection titled *No Comebacks* (1982). One of those short stories, carrying the simple title "Privilege," is a superlative example of the search for alternatives. Consider the plight of Bill Chadwick, the fictional subject in Forsyth's short story.

Bill Chadwick is awakened from a lazy Sunday morning sleep by a friend who suggests that Bill needs to obtain and read a copy of the *Sunday Courier*, which carries a story concerning the fraudulent dealings of a company that has just collapsed. Chadwick's company had business relationships with the collapsed company, and the article implies that Chadwick's company was operating a little on the shady side as well — a classic case of guilt by association.

Chadwick quickly senses the potential damage to his company and tries to see Gaylord Brent, the investigative reporter who wrote the story, hoping for a retraction. Chadwick's request for an interview is rejected by Brent, also by the paper's editor. Chadwick approaches his solicitor to examine the option of legal redress. The possibility of litigation to correct the wrongful impression of the story is an option, but not one of promise, advises the solicitor. The paper has access to expensive legal counsel. The court hearing could prove to be long term and expensive, one that might cost Chadwick and his company more than the economic damage already done by the story. Thus Chadwick is faced with an injustice, with apparently no reasonable way to have the wrong righted.

Not accepting defeat, however, Chadwick makes a trip to the library to consult the English statutes. He studies the laws of libel and finds a provision in the statute that states that anything said during the sitting of a court can be reported and published without the fear of a libel suit. This statute was designed to protect judges, witnesses, police officers, and counsel so that the truth may be pursued in the prosecution and defense of any case. Armed with this simple piece of new knowledge, Chadwick fashions his alternative and proceeds to put his plan in action.

Having failed to obtain an interview with either the reporter Gaylord Brent or the *Courier* editor, Chadwick decides to go to Brent's home and confront him. Brent answers the door but refuses again to discuss the matter, so Chadwick punches him in the nose, just hard enough to cause a nose bleed. Chadwick then summons a constable from a nearby station and returns to Brent's flat with the constable, where he confesses that he has punched Brent in the nose. With Brent's bloody nose obviously in evidence, the constable has what appears to be a simple but rather odd case of assault.

Chadwick threatens to punch Brent in the nose again, so he is duly charged and a court hearing date is set. Before the court date, Chadwick calls all other major newspapers in the city and the major TV stations and indicates that Mr. Gaylord Brent of the *Courier* will appear in court in the Case of Regina versus Chadwick. Chadwick refuses counsel, choosing to act in his own defense, and then gives this opening statement when he is called to the witness stand before the magistrate:

> Your worship, six weeks ago Mr. Gaylord Brent published this article in the newspaper for which he works, *The Sunday Courier*. In that article, Gaylord Brent perpetrated upon me a vicious and immensely damaging libel. You will observe, sir, that the article deals with a company merchandising a product and then going into liquidation, leaving a number of members of the public in forfeit of their deposits. I unfortunately was one of those businessmen who were also taken in by that company, which I, like many others, believed to be a sound company with a reliable product. The fact is, I also lost money by my mistake, but mistake it was. In this article, out of the blue, I was baselessly accused of some ill-defined complicity in the affair and accused moreover by a slovenly, lazy and incompetent hack who cannot be bothered to do his homework properly.

After a few gasps from the court and an objection from the prosecuting counsel being overruled, Chadwick continues:

> Now, had this so-called investigative journalist bothered to contact me before writing this piece of garbage, I could have produced all of my files, my accounts and my bank statements to prove to him beyond a doubt that I had been as misled as the purchasers. And had lost substantial sums into the bargain. But he could not even be bothered to contact me, although I am in the phone book and the commercial directory. It seems that behind the veneer of pretentiousness this fearless investigator is more prone to listen to bar gossip than check out the facts.

And then:

> After the appearance of this farago of lies masquerading as serious
> journalism, my business was badly affected. It was evident that some
> of my associates, unaware that Mr. Gaylord Brent's exposés emerge
> less from slogging investigation than from the bottom of the whiskey
> bottle, were even prepared to believe the libel.

By this time, reporter Brent is in a state of apoplexy in the court room.
However, the magistrate hears out the rest of the story — the unsuccessful
attempts to get an interview with Brent or the *Courier* editor, the inability
of the little man to take on the legal resources of the paper at any reasonable cost, and Brent's persistent refusal to talk with Chadwick on the fateful
Sunday morning of the nose punch. Chadwick's frustration and his "apparent momentary loss of control" in punching Brent are sympathetically
received by the court. A modest fine of 100 pounds is assessed. Chadwick
walks out of the court with only negligible financial costs, restoration of
his business's reputation, and a certain justice rendered for the careless han-
dling of the story and the personal arrogance of the reporter.

This is the story of a man thinking, who overcame seemingly overwhelming odds to produce a fresh and penetrating option where none apparently
existed. For the reader interested in a visual and more entertaining demon-
stration of this principle at work, I commend the film *Absence of Malice*
starring Paul Newman and Sally Field.

Postscript

In a spirited little essay titled "The Ups and Downs of Working Life"
(1972), former Avis Corporation president Robert Townsend notes that:

> An excellent case can be made that senior executives should not have
> offices at all. Then they would be forced to make contact with their
> fellow employees, and they might find out what their real priorities
> are. (p. 88)

In this same venue is the MBWA style (acronym for "Management by Walking About") described by Peters and Waterman in *In Search of Excellence*
in their chapter on "A Bias for Action." It means getting out in the hallways, classrooms, offices, laboratories to see what others are thinking and
feeling. It means gaining access to ideas and data that leaders cannot find
in their monthly status reports or summon from memory with their personal computers.

Not only will this inclination to action and adventure bring us the organizational intelligence we need, it will do much more, as I have tried
to suggest in this chapter. The will to action teaches the leader that:

Action informs thought, brings to light new goals and tactics that could not have been conceived without the action step.

Daring sharpens our physical and mental powers, focuses them with greater intensity on problems at hand.

Failure has a flip side, often bringing us reluctantly to new and fresh understandings about ourselves and our institutions.

A search for alternatives and persistence are the marks of the leader inclined to action and adventure.

These ideas are not usually found in the theories and principles of management texts. However, their validity and power will be affirmed by those leaders who look back on a journey of action, risk, and failure, and who look forward to the same. Apathy is the enemy of leadership, for it is the evidence of lack of caring.

Apathy is an enemy of leadership.

References

Bogue, E. Grady. *Allocation of State Funds on a Performance Criterion: The Report of the Performance Funding Project.* Nashville: The Tennessee Higher Education Commission, 1980.

Forsyth, Frederick. *No Comebacks.* New York: Viking Press, 1982.
The paraphrase of and quotation from the short story, "Privilege" is reproduced by permission of Curtis Brown, London. Copyright © 1982 by Frederick Forsyth.

Gibran, Kahlil. *Sand and Foam.* New York: Alfred A. Knopf, 1973.

Gilkey, Langdon. *The Shantung Compound.* New York: Harper & Row, 1966.

Peters, Thomas J., and Waterman, Jr., Robert H. *In Search of Excellence.* New York: Harper & Row, 1982.

Peterson, Wilferd. *The Art of Living.* New York: Simon & Schuster, 1961.

Southern Association of Colleges and Schools. *Standards of the College Delegate Assembly.* 14 December 1977.

Southern Association of Colleges and Schools. *Criteria for Accreditation.* December 1984.

Townsend, Robert. "The Ups and Downs of Working Life." In *Don't Just Do Something.* Santa Barbara, Calif.: Center for the Study of Democratic Institutions, 1972.

Chapter Four

The Instrument of Leadership Art

There are two kinds of decision; those that are expensive to change and those that are not.

> — Robert Townsend
> *Up the Organization*

And in any society those who choose the most have the most reason to feel free.

> — Harland Cleveland
> *The Future Executive*

Making decisions can make you feel tired and irritable. And making decisions can get you in trouble. To avoid both lassitude and crisis, the obvious prescription is to avoid making decisions. That too many leadership incumbents find this advice congenial is apparent enough. One of the more frequent complaints about leadership is that the leader will not make a decision. Some academic leaders are following the advice humorously given in Thomas Martin's *Malice in Blunderland* (1973), where we find the following counsel in Father Damaian Fandal's Rules for Deans (p. 90):

Rule 1: Hide!!!
Rule 2: If they find you, lie!!!

Perhaps we should not be too harsh in our judgment of the indecisive administrator. After all, revolutions have begun, wars fought, fortunes lost, careers interrupted, and lives sacrificed over decisions made — and as much over the process of decision making as over decision content. Fate can intervene to make a disastrous decision look good and a good decision disastrous. The security of indecision is appealing.

Remember, however, that indecision is a decision; it is a decision for the status quo, to do nothing. The results are described by William James:

Skepticism, then, is not avoidance of option; it is option of a certain particular kind of risk. Better risk loss of truth than chance of error. . . . It is as if a man should hesitate indefinitely to ask a certain woman to marry him because he was not perfectly sure that she would prove an angel after he brought her home. Would he not cut himself off from that particular angel possibility as decisively as if he went and married someone else? (p. 26)

Thomas Martin describes the leader who excels in indecision as "The Abominable No Man":

He says "no" because he has found that is the easiest way and because he never says anything else. Should he say "yes" he might be asked to explain the basis for his enthusiasm. Should he approve, he might be involved in work resulting from the proposal's acceptance. Should the scheme prove a failure, he might be held responsible for advocating it in the first place. But saying "no" is relatively safe. It requires no explanation because no action follows. Nor can the scheme fail because it will never be tried. . .even later acceptance of the plan need not worry the No Man unduly. He cannot be held responsible for any failure and will not be asked to aid in insuring success. Few will remember his opposition and those who do can be told that the plan in its original form was impractical and that its effective application after revision owed much to the process of healthy criticism to which it was subjected in the early stages of development. The No Man has little to lose. (pp. 76-77)

The leader can enjoy, then, a measure of security if he chooses the role of skeptic, cynic, or No Man. But he can never know achievement. Decision making, the instrument of leadership art, is the only avenue to achievement. Decision making is at once the most exciting and critical activity of leadership; it is the operational expression of one's leadership philosophy.

Less than two weeks after I assumed the chancellor's position at Louisiana State University in Shreveport, faculty of the newly established Graduate Council asked for an appointment. The policy issue posed for my consideration was who was to approve new graduate courses – the existing college and university curriculum committee, which heretofore had been doing this for all courses, or the new Graduate Council. Here was a lively decision test for the new chancellor, one that could quickly determine whether any trace of academic Solomon might be found in me or whether even the small matters would cause me to stumble, fumble, and mumble.

And here was a splendid opportunity to demonstrate my decision style. I could play the "quick-draw artist," pull my decision pistol and shoot the matter clean through with my first shot, impressing the faculty with speed and bravado, if not with results. I could play the role of "The Thinker" and strike a pose similar to Rodin's statue of the same title, suggesting perhaps some intellectual depth. I could play the role of the "therapist," listening patiently and inserting an understanding "uhhuh" from time to time, but offering no opinion. I could play the role of "jurist," searching institutional policy chronicles for some rule or precedent to apply. I could play the role of "researcher" and call for a survey of faculty opinion to ascertain the mind of the faculty on this question. I could play the role of "quantitative wizard," begging a little time to see if the issue might yield to critical path analysis or a minimum-loss decision strategy.

Though tempting, any one of these options would have been making too much of a simple matter. I remembered the last lines of this note from Chester Barnard's *The Functions of the Executive* (1938):

> The fine art of executive decision consists in not deciding questions that are not now pertinent, in not deciding prematurely, in not making decisions that cannot be made effective, and in not making decisions that others should make. (p. 194)

This decision did not belong to me. I indicated to members of the Graduate Council my intent to hold each of the three vice chancellors primarily responsible for policy, program, and personnel issues in their respective areas, and I would not deny them the opportunity to do their work. This question, I averred, fell under the domain of the vice chancellor for academic affairs. I duly referred the issue and the decision to him. And he in turn handled the matter with dispatch and sensitivity.

Some morning before your calendar gets too cluttered, wander over to the library. Take a few moments to visit with the head librarian and have a cup of coffee with members of the staff. Stop by the card catalog and pull out the "D" drawer and note how many books can be found on the topic of "Decision." Or if technology is that far along, just call up the catalog on your office personal computer. For a more dramatic impact move to the stacks and note the array of books there — from Bass's *Organizational Decision Making* to Simon's classic, *The New Science of Management Decision*. Return to your office and look through your institution's catalog to see how many courses in quantitative management and industrial engineering treat the theme of decision.

Given this extensive literature on decision making as an art form, one could argue that it is foolish to attempt any distillation of the concept. However, management as art begins with a knowledge base, as I advocate throughout this work. The artist must first know his tools. Then, by using these tools, he learns further their special uses and limitations. At the risk of oversimplification, I submit that the art of decision calls for a judicious integration of the following four questions:

What is the decision?

Who should be involved and how?

What facts and feelings should inform the decision?

What values, assumptions, and principles should guide us?

Decision Typology

In *Management Decisions by Objectives* (1969), George Odiorne proposes a typology that classifies decisions as routine, problem solving, or innovative. The department chairman scheduling courses and faculty for the next term faces a set of reasonably routine decisions, those necessary to continue the regular operation of the department. If, however, in this process he also is searching for incentives to arrange more courses in the evenings in response to recent student complaints about section availability, he could be making a problem-solving decision. And if he is planning to implement a new computer-assisted instructional program for his calculus sequence, he may be looking at an innovative decision. Here is a way of looking at decision making from this scheme:

Routine Decisions	Problem-Solving Decisions	Innovative Decisions
Carry the unit or organization forward in daily operation	Engage impediments or problems in personnel, policy, or procedure	Search for new programs, practices, or policies to improve effectiveness or to expand service

The general rule is that the base of involvement should expand as one moves from left to right on this classification scheme. Exceptions will be described in later discussion.

Another useful decision typology is suggested by Stufflebeam and colleagues (1971) in the following scheme:

	Intended	Actual
Ends	Planning Decisions to determine objectives	Recycling Decisions to judge and react to attainments
Means	Structuring Decisions to design procedures	Implementing Decisions to utilize, refine, and control procedures

What can we learn from this typology? The leader who wants things to happen must do more than simply orchestrate decisions about organizational goals or "ends." He also has a responsibility to follow through to ensure that the procedures or "means" used are adequate to attain the goals. To do this, the leader arranges for feedback to see if what was *intended* is what *actually* happened; that is, when faced with the practical realities of an organization's personnel and resources, the goals may or may not be achieved.

In *The Effective Executive* (1966) Peter Drucker offers a classification similar to the Odiorne model. He uses the term "generic" to describe those routine and repetitive decisions that can be made on the basis of a policy or principle. For example, in making promotion and tenure decisions each year, there should be a set of policies or principles to guide those decisions.

Another of Drucker's classifications is the "generic problem" decision, which is one that has occurred in other organizations but is new to a particular organization. Administrators in a university that is just beginning to offer graduate work may find decisions for admitting faculty to graduate-level status a new issue for them, but it certainly is not a new issue in higher education. Here, decision makers can and should take advantage of the experience of other institutions.

A university faced with decisions related to retrenchment may be encountering what Drucker calls a "new generic," a new class of decisions that may be repeated. Then there is the "exceptional decision" in which the probability of recurrence is very low. These are the decisions where one cannot have access to experience of others. Drucker cites the Cuban missile crisis in President Kennedy's administration as a truly exceptional decision event.

In the early Seventies, I had the opportunity to see a university president engage an exceptional decision. To protest several points of discontent with institutional policy, 100 students occupied the office of Memphis State University President Cecil C. Humphreys. The president had a spacious office, but it had not been designed to hold this number. In a climate of high tension, the president remained patient. He indicated that he would see that each of their complaints received a speedy and thorough hearing but that he would not allow them to continue occupying his office. As with so many other confrontations of that era, some faculty and staff looked on with the detached interest of parlor soldiers.

The students remained in the office. The president had them arrested, taken to the city police station, and booked. However, he had the vice president for student affairs accompany them to the station to ensure that all were treated with courtesy and released back to the university, where each one was placed on social probation. He then established a task force headed by the vice president for administration to investigate quickly and thoroughly the students' complaints and to bring him action recommendations. Here was a decision of the moment. No committees. No studies. No consultants. The president acted decisively, fairly. He let the students feel the edge of his conviction but also his compassion.

Simon (1960) has described decisions as "programmed" or "non-programmed." The director of purchasing knows when he must go to bid (programmed). The vice chancellor considering a re-organization of colleges and departments may be working a swamp with a lot of mean alligators (non-programmed). There are a number of other classification models, but our understandings will not be advanced by pressing the matter of typology further.

There is one important point before we leave this section. Too many decisions are brought to the executive and defined in terms of only two alternatives. The careless executive may not pause long enough to ask if the decision is so clearly black or white. Hiding in most decision dichotomies are other options that can be pursued.

A decade ago, when I was assistant vice president for academic affairs at Memphis State University, the vice president dispatched me to Nashville to represent the university in a new program hearing before the Tennessee Higher Education Commission, a state-level coordinating agency for higher education. On this particular day, we were proposing a bachelor's degree major in Russian.

Just as we were about to enter the hearing room, I learned that the commission's academic staff was going to recommend against our program. The conventional decision options for new programs were *approval* or *disapproval*, a clear-cut decision dichotomy. Keep in mind that the commission had only the authority to approve or disapprove; it could not terminate a program once it had begun.

As the hearing got underway with proposed new programs from other institutions, my mind began to race. How could I prevent the commission from turning us down cold? Was there an alternative to the decision dichotomy? I listened carefully to the arguments given by the academic officer of the commission — concern over possible low enrollments, limited number of faculty and need for additional faculty, doubtful employment opportunities, etc. When I rose to address the commission, I invited them to consider a third option, one never presented to the commission in past hearings. I proposed a "contingency approval."

I proposed that the commission approve the bachelor's degree in Russian on the contingency that Memphis State University would meet each of the concerns listed by the academic staff within a time-frame to be established by the commission staff — that Memphis State University would go on record as agreeing to terminate the program voluntarily if it failed to meet all of those conditions to the satisfaction of the staff. The commission bought my proposal. One of the more interesting ironies of my academic life is that within two years I had become the academic officer of the Tennessee Higher Education Commission. It became my responsibility a few years later to evaluate the contingency conditions that I originally proposed to the commission. Memphis State still has the major in Russian.

Decision Style

Who will be affected by a decision? A simple question. To neglect this question, however, is the one act most likely to torpedo the leader's flagship. The guiding principle is that those affected by a decision should have ownership in that decision. The landscape of academia is littered with the skeletal remains of ideas killed not because they lacked substance but because administrators failed to involve those affected.

Some academic administrators are prone to a heroic style of leadership, feeling that they are destined to stand above their staffs and faculties, making those difficult decisions others will not make. Commenting on this heroic style, Keller says in *Academic Strategy* (1983):

> The erosion of institutional collegiality is often combined with the long famous reluctance of most professors to come to closure, to choose priorities, or to decide anything irrevocably. (p. 172)

Having dealt with the professors, Keller then targets presidents with this indictment:

> Except among rare individuals, presidents in American higher education tend to avoid management and leadership like a poison ivy patch. (p. 172)

There are three difficulties with the heroic style of leadership. First, if you really expect that faculty and other colleagues will not take responsibility for their own welfare, you are hardly likely to insist that they do so. Second, you deny yourself access to intelligence and experience, which may save you from your own narrowness and arrogance. Finally, you will likely spend considerable time in cleaning up the debris of ill-considered decisions if you neglect the involvement of those whose welfare will be affected by decisions.

In a recent discussion over budget priorities, I listened as two faculty members from different disciplines exchanged competing views. One suggested that the university was endorsing slave labor by paying part-time English faculty our current modest stipend. The other faculty member from science suggested that this was the most obvious and fairest way to achieve necessary efficiencies in a time of tight budgets. Will we raise the pay of our part-time faculty before we increase travel for regular faculty?

What of other resource tensions? Will we build the performing arts center on our campus before the library addition? Will we add additional faculty next year before we add another counselor or security officer? Will we squeeze money from the equipment budget to provide a little more for salary increases? Will we start the new master's degree just approved, even though we cannot afford to give the faculty release time for graduate course preparation and research?

As chancellor, I can answer these questions. And in a way I will eventually be responsible for all of them. But these questions of purpose and priority are matters of community concern. They deserve consideration in a variety of forums that will encourage both ownership and decision responsibility.

51

The managerial mind, then, is one that insists on cultivation of community, calling colleagues to the discomforting challenge of discerning purpose and priorities. It is a mind that brings patience and perspective to the dissent that is inevitable when clarifying purposes and establishing ownership of those purposes. It is also a mind that is marked by decision courage when that is required. Any administrator worthy of the role, at one time or another, will find himself in lonely vigil when facing a situation requiring decision courage. The willingness to stand for what we know to be right, for high standards of performance, for integrity in both educational and management stewardship is the mark of decision courage.

A few years ago, a college dean friend confronted his entire faculty with a pleasant display of courage. In his college of education, the faculty had been requiring all of its doctoral students to take approximately one-third of their course work in supporting academic fields outside the college of education. The sustaining principle was that such course work enlarged and strengthened the doctoral program.

After a few years, the demand for advanced graduate work in the college of education began to soften, and the faculty saw both credit hours and faculty positions beginning to slip away. Convening in somber session, the faculty agreed that it made good academic sense to terminate the out-of-college requirement and bring all those graduate credit hours back home to the college of education.

My friend the dean dissented. He indicated that their decision was transparent and unworthy and that he would neither sanction nor approve their recommendation. This was a lonely and courageous act. I think it was also a correct act.

We are left with artistic choice, then, on whether we choose the "participative" or "heroic" model of decision making. And that choice turns on a careful analysis of decision climate and values. Let me save for the moment the discussion about values and consider briefly those factors related to the decision climate.

The heroic model may prove the most appropriate when:

Time or resources do not permit extended consultation or involvement.

The decision is relatively routine and does not affect the personal welfare of faculty or staff in a dramatic way.

Those affected by the decision abdicate their responsibility for involvement.

The participative model yields a decision that the leader judges to be harmful or incorrect. For example, the illustration previously cited for the dean of education.

When choosing participative models, we first need to recognize the variety of participative models. A full franchise model allows every affected individual to participate in the decision. A representative model permits efficiency by having selected individuals represent a constituency. A synectic model is one in which members are selected not so much for their functional expertise but because they bring fresh perspective, even naiveté. A variant of the functional model is the "consultant" model in which external consultants are brought in to the decision process because of their special expertise and their objectivity as external evaluators.

Consider the decision challenge facing a college dean who believes his departmental structure is in need of overhaul but who faces an entrenched inertia of personnel and policy. For him to take the matter in hand directly could be a high-risk affair. But if faculty are invited to participate in the selection of the consultant team to assist in restructuring the college, then all parties have the advantage of external expertise, which has been jointly selected.

Consultants extract no decision freedom from responsible academic managers, although they can be seen as a threat to the insecure academic manager. Consultants also can serve a therapeutic function. Staff often will talk more freely and openly with a neutral third party. However, this therapeutic value can backfire if embittered and cynical staff members convey a negative or unhealthy climate by being strongly vocal while others are relatively quiet.

Decision — Fact and Feeling

The conventional notion of decision making is that one starts with the facts, looks at the alternatives, and then chooses the most satisfying alternative. Scholar and practitioner know, however, that a decision often starts with opinion. Many of the major policy decisions that affect our institutions are not based on objective and rational analyses. They often involve political considerations and personality quirks of the most astonishing nature. And it is not so much the facts themselves that count as it is the interpretation of those facts. I have often wondered what was going on inside the corporate board room when Ford Motors readied the Edsel automobile for production and market. I suspect all the trend charts had a positive slope. Here are three vignettes on the role of fact and feeling in decisions in academic settings.

Shortly after I was appointed director of institutional research at Memphis State University, the president dispatched me as a facilities missionary to Manning Hall, at that time the domain of the major science disciplines of the university. The president's interest lay in the possibility of moving a newly established nursing program into Manning Hall in order to free up some other critically needed space. A quick perusal of the room scheduling and utilization chart revealed that many of the classrooms then devoted to physics were lightly utilized, perhaps one or two three-hour classes per week. A careful scheduling, it appeared, could free several general classrooms. If one were willing to probe further, there might be gains to be had in laboratories as well.

What this neat piece of computer analysis failed to reveal, however, was the volatile disposition and proprietary interests of the campus's most celebrated and vocal chairman. I marshalled my most tactful approach, but had hardly begun the conversation on the possibility of freeing classrooms for nursing, when the chairman moved quickly through countdown and launched from his desk chair up through the ceiling. When he again settled behind his desk, I was declared persona non grata. Shortly after my visit, the chairman visited each of the classrooms in question, depositing in each a piece of equipment from the atomic and nuclear physics lab — a scaler counter here, a Wilson cloud chamber there, a Millikan oil drop apparatus in the next. And on each door he posted the bright yellow and red poster "Danger — Radiation."

Fortunately, this same chairman and other departmental colleagues had taught me well in my undergraduate physics, and I didn't need an advanced degree in physics to see through this ploy. The president forced the issue on the hunch that the chairman, given a little time, might find the presence of a lively group of nursing faculty and students a salutary addition to the classrooms of the science building. The president was correct. Here was a decision where elementary facts sustained an effective decision in the face of an imposing authority figure.

A friend who is chairman of a university sociology department began to worry about the quality of some of his master's degree graduates. After reviewing the qualifying exams for the last two graduating classes for the master's degree, he was chagrined to find that student performance on several of these qualifying exams bordered on what he charitably described as barely literate. To check his impression of graduate standards, he asked the graduate dean to select several highly respected graduate faculty from the departments of psychology, educational foundations, English, history, and anthropology to review these exams. For several of the exams, this ad hoc review panel agreed without dissent that the students in question would not have graduated had the exam been the major criterion of performance and competence.

The chairman then matched the exams against the grades of the students and confronted his graduate faculty with the results. His question was a simple one. How was it that master's students, whose written performance on the department's major quality assurance exit instrument was so miserable, could have completed many, in some cases most, of their courses with grades of A? This quality assurance venture so alarmed and impressed the graduate dean that the matter of cross-departmental review of qualifying exams became a topic of lively discussion on the next Graduate Council agenda.

Several years ago, as assistant vice president for academic affairs at Memphis State University, I participated in annual budget reviews for departments. In one of the hearings, a department chairman requested that several new faculty be added to reduce the extraordinarily large classes, which his department had obligingly accepted in order to accommodate the dramatic enrollment increase in recent years. Those sitting around the hearing table — the dean, the vice president — were ready to write in two or three new positions, when a staff colleague across the table asked to say a word.

Thumbing through several pages of data, this staff person indicated that the credit hour production profile for this particular department had remained level for the last five years (this was a time when university enrollments were growing but not in this department), that graduate activity had actually shown a slight decline, and that average class sizes in this department were actually slightly below similar departments. Simple data. Yet useful to the decision at hand.

The lesson from these vignettes is clear: the administrator who attempts to operate any unit or institution without adequate facts performs a disservice. One of the more arresting questions that can be put to any education administrator is this: What information indicators do you need to judge the educational and administrative effectiveness of your unit or institution? Enrollment, credit hour production, and graduate trends? Proportion of budget devoted to primary programs compared to administration and support services? Student performance/outcomes and opinion/satisfaction data? Promotion, tenure, age profiles for faculty and staff? The wise education leader needs facts for decisions in these areas.

Occasionally, however, one can have the facts and still not have a clear direction for decisions. Many decisions do not yield to the analytical neatness of an "IF" statement in a well-written FORTRAN or BASIC program statement. If the department is 80% tenured, what does that fact portend for the tenure decision on a bright and energetic young assistant professor. Is it up and out for the sake of the tenure quota? Or will the potential of that young talent warrant setting the tenure percentage aside? What if the facts reveal potential and dramatic savings for a library security system, an automatic irrigation system for the campus, or a computer-managed energy conservation system? The facts by themselves do not indicate whether these expenditures are more important to the future of the campus than an additional security office or new radio equipment. Here is where the participative decision models discussed earlier can begin to be helpful.

When weighing the influence of opinion and feelings in decisions, a leader will first want to avoid the tendency to impute representativeness to loudness of voice. Second, the leader will want to realize that decision trust is promoted by personal contact. It is easy to be suspicious of someone whom you do not know. A little time taken to cultivate the acquaintance of those who will be making decisions about the welfare of your unit or institution can have a positive payoff.

The discussion of decision making to this point neglects the entire field of decision theory. I refer to a range of decision models, consensual strategies, and statistical techniques; for example, such decision approaches as Synectics (Gordon 1961), Brainstorming (Osborn 1963), and the Delphi Technique (Dalkey 1969), also such techniques as Critical Path Analysis and Minimum Loss strategies. Readers interested in summary treatments of these approaches to decision are referred to an earlier work by Irwin Bross (1953) and a more recent work by Jerome Braverman (1980). For examples of these decision tools applied to college and university settings, see Bogue (1968), Parden (1972), Lawrence and Service (1977), and Gulko and Hussain (1971).

Decision Philosophy

Decision is the operational test of leadership philosophy. In decisions are found the fundamental issues of risk, trust, professional competence, and personal strength. What holds true for the philosophy of the individual leader holds for his unit or organization. One of the newer books on management, William Ouchi's *Theory Z* (1981), emphasizes the importance of both a company and individual philosophy. The first lesson of Theory Z is trust:

> the basic mechanism of control in a Japanese company is embodied in a philosophy of management. This philosophy, an implicit theory of the firm, describes the objectives and the procedures to move towards them. These objects represent the values of the owners, employees, customers, and government regulators. (p. 41)

Ouchi then goes on to suggest in another chapter that:

> popular belief aside, philosophy and business are the most compatible of bedfellows. To the extent that practical no-nonsense business decisions come from a consistent, integrated set of ideas, they are more likely to prove successful in the long run. (p. 131)

In yet another contemporary volume, *Decision Making at the Top* (1983), Donaldson and Lorsch devote an entire chapter to the importance of the belief system of organizational executives. Titled "The Psychology of Executive Choice," the chapter emphasizes the finding that "these interrelated beliefs act as a filter through which management perceives the realities facing its firm" (p. 79). Leadership beliefs about organizational goals and environment, risk taking, means and ends, colleague competence, and role not only perceive but construct reality. This is a point earlier emphasized in Chapters One and Two, and one that I will be returning to throughout the book.

At Louisiana State University in Shreveport, the faculty and the administration have fashioned a long-range planning process, the origins of which

56

are described in Chapter Three. Each academic and administrative unit in the university has built a set of short-range objectives and longer-range goals. These objectives/goals are then linked with individual administrator and faculty goals. At this point, the planning process is still in its formative stages, and by no means would it escape critical commentary from a planning expert. For example, we have yet to learn how to perform the linkages of the university's goals to individual goals; and we have not adequately developed time-lines and resource demands for each of the objectives. One thing we have done, however, is to factor from the unit plans an umbrella statement of institutional goals. In a preface statement to those larger goals we have published this brief statement of university philosophy, which is reprinted below.

STATEMENT OF UNIVERSITY GOALS 1984-87
LOUISIANA STATE UNIVERSITY IN SHREVEPORT

PURPOSES OF THIS STATEMENT

The purposes of this statement are . . .
> To inform external publics of major university goals.
> To promote awareness and ownership of these goals.
> To strengthen commitment toward achievement of goals.
> To provide a basis for review and reform of university mission.

UNIVERSITY PLANNING

These more general goals represent a vision shared by faculty and administration of the University. These are not the only goals on which faculty and staff are at work. More comprehensive and specific statements of activity and aspiration are found in the yearly plans of the colleges and administrative units.

These goals represent statements of intent. Achievement of some goals requires only initiative and commitment while many others will obviously require the acquisition of financial resources. Operating on the conviction that ideas and initiative do not guarantee achievement but are still the foundation for achievement, the university faculty and staff will make every effort to obtain the funds — public and private — necessary to achieve these goals.

A PHILOSOPHIC COMMITMENT

We will honor the university's primary mission of instruction, expecting competent and caring performance in the classroom and in service to students as the first call on faculty talent and devotion. Beyond this primary expectation, we will expect faculty involvement in activities of university service, community service, professional service and research appropriate to their interests and talent.

We will meet the public service expectation of the University by developing programs of continuing education, leadership development, applied research, and consultation appropriate to the needs of the urban and surrounding community.

We will strive to nurture the mission of research, especially in those program areas where there are graduate programs, encouraging faculty interest in research and supporting the acquisition of funds to underwrite research.

We will value optimistic and forward-looking vision over procedure and policy, and we will be willing to dare and to risk, not being bound by precedent, accepting the possibility of failure that accompanies the possibility of achievement.

We will treat each one served by the University — and our colleagues — with dignity, rendering instructional and administrative service marked by courtesy and competence.

We will be effective and efficient stewards of the resources entrusted to our care, and we will exert our imagination and initiative in bringing private support to the university, as a means of enriching the quality of program opportunity and performance.

UNIVERSITY GOALS

Strengthen Existing Programs

Fully staff and support existing instructional and support programs.

Expand and strengthen public service programs in . . .

Red River Regional Studies

Business and Economic Research

International Studies

Expand and strengthen internship and cooperative education experiences for University students, as an instrument for graduating students who have experienced both theoretical and applied issues in their respective fields of study.

Secure private funding that will provide faculty and staff salary supplements, with the goal of placing faculty and staff average salaries in the "above-average" range for peer institutions.

Secure private funding that will support five Distinguished Professorial appointments with an average annual supplement of $4,000 to $5,000.

Improve Quality Assurance

Achieve accreditation for undergraduate and graduate programs in the College of Business.

Achieve accreditation for the Master of Education degree and Specialist of Psychology degree in the College of Education.

Establish a quality assurance program that will yield recurrent data on student satisfaction and student performance on measures of general education achievement and major field achievement.

Initiate an evaluation and review effort to monitor existing programs on a regular basis.

Establish an Ad Hoc Task Force on Resource Utilization as a means of finding ways to improve the effectiveness/efficiency of resource application in both primary programs and support services.

Establish New Degree and Public Service Programs

Establish an evening undergraduate program leading to the Bachelor of Science in Engineering.

Establish a Master of Biological Sciences.

Establish a Master of Computer Science.

Establish a Financial Service Center in the College of Business.

Establish a Science Education Center in the College of Science.

Strengthen Administrative and Student Services

Implement a more complete diagnostic and referral service in career assessment and planning, for both university students and as a community/educational service.

Improve administrative service effectiveness and efficiency by continued automation of services with special focus in business, admission-registration, and university relations areas.

Implement a program of administrative services evaluation that will involve survey/questionnaire approaches and a peer team visit.

Improve Facilities and Plant Operation

Complete planning and construction of the Noel Memorial Library.

Renovate the Science Building, following relocation of administrative offices.

Obtain private funding for a Fine Arts Building.

Renovate the old library.

Acquire additional land for the University.

The development of an organizational philosophy is no sterile matter. For example, a registrar or business office committed to a "service" ethic, of which we will say more in Chapter Seven, will show a different public face to faculty and students because that ethic is given both philosophical and operational allegiance. Finally, it is critically important that the leader fashion a personal philosophy. When an angry student, faculty member, board member, or member of the community shows up in front of your desk or on the phone, it is too late to fashion a philosophy. Your values are going to express themselves in that moment.

As I reflect on the concepts presented in this chapter, here are the philosophic anchors worthy of serious reflection by leaders:

- Concentrate on the exceptional decisions and leave routine decisions to others.
- Work to see that your unit or institution develops a philosophy that will guide decision and create a unit or institutional spirit/ethic.
- Insist that each officer reporting to you accept and discharge responsibility for decision within his or her position.
- Invest others with your trust. Give them the freedom to make mistakes.
- Make changes in personnel where poor judgment or no judgment causes you to do your job *and* someone else's job.
- Look for decision alternatives where none are suggested. Be wary of decision dichotomies.
- Remain sensitive to the variety of options for participative decision making.
- Adjust decision style to decision type and climate.
- Bring both fact and feeling to focus on decision.
- Remember that volume and frequency of comment do not always correspond with accuracy or representativeness.
- Get to know those who will make decisions about your institutional or unit welfare. It is easy to mistrust those we don't know.

And the most important counsel is this. Test and clarity values now. There won't be time when you are put to the decision test. Decision is the operational test of your leadership philosophy — not the one you intend, but the one you have.

Indecision is an enemy of leadership.

60

References

Barnard, Chester I. *The Functions of the Executive*. Cambridge, Mass.: Harvard University Press, 1938.

Bass, Bernard M. *Organizational Decision Making*. Homewood, Ill.: Richard D. Irwin, 1983.

Bogue, E.G. "Application of a Minimum Loss Decision Strategy in the Selection of Cutoff Points in College and University Admissions." *College and University* (Winter 1968): 131-42.

Braverman, Jerome D. *Management Decision Making*. New York: AMACOM, 1980.

Bross, Irwin D.J. *Design for Decision*. New York: The Free Press, 1953.

Dalkey, N.C. *The Delphi Method: An Experimental Study of Group Opinion*. Santa Monica, Calif.: The RAND Corporation, 1969.

Donaldson, Gordan, and Lorsch, Jay N. *Decision Making at the Top: Shaping of Strategic Decisions*. New York: Basic Books, 1983.

Drucker, Peter F. *The Effective Executive*. New York: Harper & Row, 1966.

Gordon, William J.J. *Synectics*. New York: Harper & Row, 1961.

Gulko, Warren W., and Hussain, K.M. *A Resource Requirement Prediction Model (RRPM-1): An Introduction to the Model*. Boulder, Colo.: National Center for Higher Education Management Systems, 1971.

James, William. *The Will to Believe*. New York: Dover, 1956.

Keller, George. *Academic Strategy: The Management Revolution in American Higher Education*. Baltimore: Johns Hopkins University Press, 1983.

Lawrence, G. Ben, and Service, Allan L. *Quantitative Approaches to Higher Education Management*. ERIC/Higher Education Research Report No. 4. Washington, D.C.: American Association for Higher Education, 1977.

Martin, Thomas L. *Malice in Blunderland*. New York: McGraw-Hill, 1973.

Odiorne, George S. *Management Decisions by Objectives*. Englewood Cliffs, N.J.: Prentice-Hall, 1969.

Osborn, A.F. *Applied Imagination: Principles and Procedures of Creative Problem Solving*. New York: Scribner's, 1963.

Ouchi, William. *Theory Z: How American Business Can Meet the Japanese Challenge*. Reading, Mass.: Addison-Wesley, 1981.

Parden, Robert J. "The Delphi Technique Modified for Establishing Institutional Priorities as a Prerequisite to Resource Allocation." In *Reformation and Reallocation in Higher Education: 12th Annual Forum of the Association for Institutional Research*, edited by Clifford T. Stewart. 1972.

Simon, Herbert A. *The New Science of Management Decision*. New York: Harper & Row, 1960.

Stufflebeam, Daniel I., et al. *Educational Evaluation and Decision Making*. Bloomington, Ind.: Phi Delta Kappa, 1971.

Chapter Five

The Timid Philosophers

What would happen to a business enterprise that had no information on sales volume or on profits or losses? No corporate executive in his right mind would consider approaching his board of directors unless he first had a clear picture of the company's financial condition. Yet, lacking any systematic information on what students are learning or how they feel about their educational experience, college administrators routinely make recommendations to their trustees for changes in faculty, staff, physical plant, or even academic programs.

— Alexander W. Astin

In measuring things that can be counted or expressed in quantifiable terms, we are led unawares to the grand illusion — that only the measurable really matters.

— Harold Enarson

Several years ago I read *To Teach, To Love* (1973) by Kentucky author Jesse Stuart. In the preface, Mr. Stuart remarked that "We never called our kids from the Kentucky hills culturally deprived, though many of their folks couldn't read or write; we just taught them and they learned" (p. 7). I like that. This is a quality expectation.

We have difficulty with the concept of quality assurance in educational institutions. Journal articles and convention speeches warn us against simple-minded approaches to student outcomes. Regional accrediting associations wonder whether they can, whether they should, ask their member institutions to know as much about their students on exit as on entry. Faculties hesitate at the suggestion of program evaluation efforts. College presidents and other academic administrators often engage in lively and labored debate over whether you can assess quality before you define it, often concluding that you can neither define nor assess quality.

But if you can't define it and you can't assess it, does it exist? This is where Robert Pirsig left us several years ago:

> Quality. . .you know what it is, yet you don't know what it is. But that's self-contradictory. But some things *are* better than others, that

is, they have more quality. But when you try to say what the quality is, apart from the things that have it, it all goes *poof*! There's nothing to talk about. But if you can't say what quality is, how do you know what it is, or how do you know that it even exists? If no one knows what it is, then for all practical purposes it doesn't exist at all. But for all practical purposes it really *does* exist. What else are the grades based on? Why else would people pay fortunes for some things and throw others in the trash pile? Obviously some things are better than others...but what's the 'betterness?'.... So round and round you go, spinning mental wheels and nowhere finding any place to get traction. What the hell is quality? What is it? (p. 184)

We know! We know when we are challenging talent and when we are not. We know when teaching is demeaning to bright and lively spirits. We know when classroom climates are never sparked by the exhilarating and exciting clash of minds and ideas. We know when we are treating our students with an arrogance unworthy of those who hold the human spirit and mind in trust. And we know when programs are cheating students of their potential.

This chapter is a call to action regarding our responsibility for quality assurance. I first want to say a word about the forces that keep us from constructive ventures in quality assurance. By means of a few illustrations, I hope to show why we need a little more action.

Impeding and Immobilizing Forces

Purpose and performance — those responsible for leadership of education institutions share the same obligations as leaders in private-sector enterprise. "What business are we in?" and "How are we doing?" are the two most important questions — and often the most neglected — in any enterprise. Answering these questions for education institutions is complex work.

Educational Purpose. When one asks questions of educational effectiveness, is it reasonable to insist that judgments of quality reflect some benchmark of expectation, some consensus on purpose? Do our colleges serve:

Economic purposes — to prepare graduates for meaningful work?

Social purposes — to promote unity in our society?

Political purposes — to sustain democracy?

Ethical purposes — to transmit values?

Legal purposes — to ensure justice?

Personal purposes — to promote individual fulfillment?

A college graduate who can read, write, and think has been educated to serve each of these purposes. But the question of purpose becomes more complex, however, when one considers the dilemma facing a college president and faculty confronted with external pressures to expand remedial programs and at the same time to obtain accreditation for a college of business.

Definition of Quality. Exactly what constitutes educational quality? Philosophers suggest that quality is real but, like love, cannot be measured or assessed. Those who judge quality on the basis of reputation already know that Harvard University has higher quality than Bossier Parish Community College in my community, even though these two institutions serve different purposes and student clientele. Is bigger better? Those who like to define quality by size might believe that Louisiana State University in Baton Rouge (enrollment approximately 30,000) is a higher quality institution than Louisiana State University in Shreveport (enrollment approximately 5,000). In truth, however, each of these institutions can have – and should have – a high quality reputation and record based on its respective mission.

Those who define quality in terms of outcomes are impressed with an institution whose teacher education and accounting graduates consistently score well on the National Teacher Examination and the CPA exam. Those who want to define quality in value-added terms focus not on outcomes but on growth or improvement. However, if school or college graduates have shown a good deal of intellectual growth and still cannot read, write, or compute, the quality question is left dangling.

Not an idle issue in quality assessment is the matter of reputation. When senior personnel executives in some of America's largest industrial, banking, and utility firms were asked to identify the nation's top-ranked undergraduate business schools, they named Harvard, Stanford, Columbia, University of Chicago, and Northwestern – no surprises on this list (Webster 1981). Neither of our two fine institutions in Shreveport, Centenary College and LSU-Shreveport, made the list. However, it should be noted that none of the above highly ranked universities have *undergraduate* programs in business. Reputations do not always match realities!

Performance Evidence. What evidence must be assembled to ascertain whether a college or university is doing its job? Will we use a criterion-referenced or a norm-referenced test? That is, do we want to know how our college seniors are doing in basic intellectual skills on the basis of predetermined criteria of performance, or on the basis of comparison with state, regional, or national population? How about opinion polls? Do we want to know what our education "customers" think about their educational experience? How might these opinions be related to what they actually learned? Or how about performance on professional examinations? If we measure the quality of a law school on how many students pass the bar exam but bar standards are raised to limit the number of attorneys admitted to practice, does this mean a law school has become less effective?

Evaluation Method. Once we have agreed on what evidence to assemble, how will we analyze that evidence? Scientists will want an experiment and philosophers a logical argument. Lawyers will want an adversarial hearing and theologians a reference to scripture. Sociologists will want an opinion poll and artists a panel of judges. Engineers will want a systems study and economists a cost/benefit analysis. Given these different conceptual vehicles, we should not find it surprising that it is difficult to obtain consensus on means for evaluating quality and effectiveness.

Mission Diversity. There will be little argument that the mission of Oberlin College differs in significant ways from that of West Point or that both of these will have a mission different from that of Evergreen State College. It is often argued that it is no more possible to evaluate the quality of institutions with such mission diversity than it is to evaluate the quality of a Chevrolet compared to a Rolls Royce. Pursuing the automobile analogy, Abernathy et al. (1983), in *Industrial Renaissance*, have this to say about quality assurance in the automobile business:

> Many domestic consumers regard a car with a luxurious interior, stately dimensions, and "boulevard" ride as being of high quality; others attach that label to a car with functional interior, aerodynamic styling, quick acceleration, and responsive handling. How to choose between them? In point of fact, there is no reasonable way to do so, for these cars were designed for quite different purposes and were intended to satisfy quite different sets of preferences. Evaluations of quality based on workmanship, reliability, and durability, however, would apply to both cars. It requires no leap of faith to believe that most consumers would view a car with obvious streaks in the paint job, windows that do not roll all the way up, doors that do not hang right, an engine that leaks oil, and an electrical system that fails after 500 miles, as being of lower quality than a competitor's product without these failings. (p. 64)

What are the education equivalents of "workmanship, reliability, and durability"? If a student earns a bachelor's degree from either Oberlin or West Point and cannot write a decent sentence or paragraph, is this a quality assurance issue of common concern? If a student graduates from Louisiana State University in Shreveport, a public university, or nearby Centenary College, a private liberal arts college, and cannot add and subtract simple signed numbers, is this a quality assurance challenge to both institutions?

The diversity of institutions and programs within those institutions notwithstanding, many faculties have yet to grapple with the quality assurance question of what skills and knowledge they want each of their degree recipients to possess. This is an issue I shall return to later in this discussion.

Mission Distortion. Narrow definitions of educational quality or effectiveness may pervert the educational process and distort the educational mission of our colleges and universities. Take, for example, the teaching-to-the-test syndrome. If the principal criterion of educational quality is a high score on a standardized test, then faculty may be encouraged to forsake the benefits of other intellectual inquiry in order to focus only on the concepts to be assessed by the test. Colleges and universities, like some profit-sector enterprises, may turn out to be very efficient in accomplishing unworthy or narrowly conceived goals. This is the educational equivalent of maximizing short-term profits to the detriment of long-term organizational health in the business sector. In his book *Megatrends* (1982), John Naisbitt describes this as "making the current quarter look good at the expense of the future" (p. 79).

Information Abuse. Will board members and legislators abuse performance data? Will they fail to understand the finer distinctions of quality definition, the limitations of our instruments and data? And will they use data in a punitive way? Some faculties and academic administrators see this as a danger in quality assurance efforts.

These anxieties are not unlike those that emerged when states first began to use formula funding policies. At that time, the concern was that board members, legislators, and other policymakers would insist that institutions conform to the lowest cost profile. That abuse did not materialize in any significant way that I can discern from experience and the literature, and I really do not believe we will see any dramatic or widespread abuse of performance information. Perhaps the challenge is not to fear abuse but to use performance data to better inform interested publics.

Evaluation Ideology. Evaluation is by definition a judgmental process. From our discussion this far, it will be obvious that judgments are involved in most every step of the educational quality assurance process: in defining educational purposes, in collecting performance evidence, and in using appropriate evaluation models. Thus, the ideology of both professionals and laymen can complicate the approach to quality assurance. Evidence and statistics are not without emotion. At the school or college level, the same student performance on standardized examinations of basic skills can be:

1. attacked on the basis of social or financial discrimination;
2. cited as evidence of the need for additional financial, personnel, or facility resources;
3. heralded as the result of effective teaching;
4. used as support for the conviction that teacher/administrator expectations are as important as buildings and budgets.

Ideology attaches ethical, social, political, and financial dimensions to evidence.

In the early 1970s, two evaluation teams of the then new children's TV program "Sesame Street" came to different conclusions. One investigation team found the show to be effective in that children who watched the program were generally more knowledgeable in those areas the program stressed: classification, puzzles, knowledge of body parts, letters, numbers, etc. Another investigation team found that the program should be discontinued because it widened the gap between advantaged and disadvantaged children, since more middle-class children watched the show than poor children did (Messick 1975). Same data, different ideology!

Voluntary Professional Accreditation. Both professionals and laymen have looked to accrediting associations to enforce quality assurance in American education. Accreditation historically has been viewed as education's "Good Housekeeping Seal of Approval." Among the kinds of evidence traditionally assembled to judge quality when accrediting schools and colleges are the following: student-faculty ratios, percentage of faculty with advanced degrees, average faculty salaries, expenditures per student, number of volumes in library, and condition of physical plant. There are, however, stresses in the fabric of our faith in accrediting associations.

David Webster (1981) has described the inadequacies of some conventional indicators of college quality:

> one frequently used "objective" measure of ranking institutions and individual departments was by the percentage of their faculty, or their senior faculty, who possessed Ph.D.'s. Around 1970, one well-known department would have been ranked quite low in such a quality ranking — fully three of its senior professors had no Ph.D. One had a law degree, one had only an M.Ed., and the third had only a B.A. Yet these three members of Harvard's Social Relations Department — David Riesman, Christopher Jencks, and Erik Erikson — might possibly have been better scholars and teachers than some professors who did possess earned doctorates. (p. 22)

It is not that these are not valid indicators; the problem is that institutions with a good "pedigree" on these indicators may not always match pedigree with performance, while institutions without the pedigree sometimes demonstrate good performance by their graduates.

When certain unsavory educational practices proceed under the seal of accreditation, when an institution borders on the verge of financial or educational collapse with the flag of accreditation still flying, when accrediting associations are strangely quiet while both education and integrity issues swirl about college athletic programs, then laymen are certain to question the value of accreditation as an indicator of quality assurance.

New and unconventional colleges are saying to the accrediting associations, "Evaluate us on the performance of our graduates and not on how large the library is." Traditional educators fight back by suggesting that if you want to be accredited as a school or college, then you have to look like a school or college — and that includes having a reasonably well-stocked library.

The Uncongenial Agenda

Faced with these impressive philosophic and technical barriers, our tendency is to debate the quality question into oblivion and simply do nothing. However, there is a growing public impatience with such inertia. Come with me for a brief trip to the imaginary state of New Winston. Several vignettes will illustrate different forms of a common problem.

Admissions Standards at Harpeth State College. A regional college of approximately 8,000 FTE students located in the city of Mullins Chapel, Harpeth State College implemented last year an "experimental" admissions policy that departed from a modestly selective admissions policy formerly in effect. In past years, students could qualify for admission to Harpeth by satisfying specified standards for high school GPA's and College Board scores. The new policy admits students of very high risk on the usual indicators of academic readiness. While open to the educational and philosophical arguments for such a policy, legislators from the Mullins Chapel area are curious about its timing. The policy was implemented the year after the college experienced its first enrollment decline in 30 years.

Innovative Credits at Crendler State Community College. Across the city, a sister institution, Crendler State Community College, has enjoyed the unhappy privilege of appearing on the front page of the evening newspaper three nights in a row. According to the story, the college has been awarding academic credit for participation in National Guard drill. Crendler does not have any program remotely related to military science, and the National Guard folks were not even aware they were getting credit. To his close friends, the dean of instruction at CSCC indicates that this was an attempt to compensate for the loss of students to Harpeth's new "open" admissions policy.

Graduate Admissions at the University of New Winston. In the midstate capital city of Regina stands the University of New Winston, the oldest and largest university in the state system. The psychology department there has just reduced the Graduate Record Exam (GRE) scores required for admission to doctoral work from a threshold of 1,150 to 900. Proud of its past adherence to a high cutoff score on the GRE as an important indicator of departmental quality, the department now finds it philosophically and educationally sound to admit students well below that original threshold. Once again, however, the timing is a bit awkward. The policy was implemented just a few months after the department surrendered two faculty positions because of declining enrollments.

Retention Standards at Guyman State University. In the northeast corner of the state lies Guyman State University. In checking student grade records against fee reports, a state financial auditor accidentally discovered that several students were apparently ineligible to still be enrolled. A full-scale audit of the institution's records revealed that more than 1,500 enrolled students were academically ineligible — according to the institution's retention policy. Further investigation revealed that the university had not executed its retention policy for the past two years.

More Innovative Credits at Tellico Community College. In the small southwest community of Tellico, Tellico Community College shares with Crendler State Community College the unhappy condition of being exposed in a statewide news story on educational standards in the state's community colleges. Crendler's generosity in awarding credit for National Guard drill was exceeded by Tellico's awarding credit in dietetics and personal health for its once-a-month luncheon for senior citizens.

Off-Campus Education at New Winston State University. In the small city of Midland, a master's level off-campus course in criminal justice convenes in the local high school each Monday night. The educational experience can be fairly described as the sharing of sermonettes and experience vignettes among the professor and students. No reading is required or encouraged. No clinical or field experience is involved. No written work or other expression of intellectual independence is required. The only evaluation in the course, of any form, is the final examination, a 25-item, true-false test followed by a class dinner at a local restaurant.

An Evening MBA Program at Richland State University. Commuters leaving trains at Union Station in Richland are treated to the new "marketing" in higher education in the form of a large billboard inviting them to explore an evening MBA program at Richland State University. Admission to the new evening MBA program requires a bachelor's degree and sufficient funds to pay the tuition. Faculty teaching in the evening MBA program are the same as those in the day programs, complemented by some adjunct faculty from the Richland business community. There is no difference between the two degrees in course descriptions, the appearance of the diploma, the course delivery, the requirements for the degree, the way in which the degrees are posted to the student's academic record, or in any other public description or reporting of the degree. But, no matter what their scholastic record, students completing work in the evening program may not transfer to the day program unless they achieve a specified cutoff score on the Graduate Management Admissions Test (GMAT). Meanwhile, professors in the business school are teaching their students a course in business ethics.

The seven vignettes described above are not hypothetical or manufactured!

Timid Philosophers

I have this private theory that public-sector executives too often are timid philosophers, that the only performance indicator they are comfortable with is growth. The only way they can feel good about their institutions and themselves is to get bigger. When asked about what the growth limit should be, glazed expressions cross their faces, suggesting that this is a worthy question to be taken up by the next president.

When we are timid philosophers, when we let fuzzy thinking and faint hearts keep us from serious attempts to evaluate our education programs and policies, we are inviting others to evaluate higher education on an agenda

69

potentially uncongenial to academic life. Those who are willing to surrender the offensive are destined to play a defensive game.

It is clear that elementary and secondary education in our nation has come through a period when schools and school leaders were often on the quality assurance defensive. Might this happen to higher education? The *Chronicle of Higher Education* (12 September 1984) carried this front-page headline: "National Concern over Educational Quality Seen Spreading from Schools to Colleges." The Study Group on the Conditions of Excellence in American Higher Education issued its report in October 1984. That report carried this note on "Assessment and Feedback":

> Faculty and academic deans should design and implement a systematic program to assess the knowledge, capacities, and skills developed in students by academic and co-curricular programs.

In the first week of February 1984, I received several unexpected phone calls from local news reporters and was visited by one TV crew. They sought my reactions to an Associated Press release that featured quality rankings of Louisiana colleges and universities as reported in *The Gourman Report* (1983).

The 4 February 1984 *Shreveport Journal* carried the following profile extracted from *The Gourman Report*, which purports to be a qualitative assessment of all undergraduate education in the U.S.

**Academic Ratings of Undergraduate Programs
in Louisiana Universities from the Gourman Report**

Tulane	4.53
LSU-Baton Rouge	4.35
LSU-Shreveport	3.38
University of New Orleans	3.30
Louisiana Tech	3.20
Southwestern	3.18
Loyola	3.17
Nicholls State	3.16
McNeese	3.15
Northeast	3.14
Northwestern	3.12
Southeastern	3.10
Centenary	3.06
Xavier	2.95
Southern University	2.90
Louisiana College	2.89
St. Mary's Dominican	2.81
Dillard	2.78
Holy Cross	2.70
Grambling	2.69
Southern University-New Orleans	2.68

At first glance, it would have been easy for me to argue for a certain validity to these ratings, since my institution, LSU-Shreveport, is the newest four-year institution in Louisiana and was ranked third out of 21 institutions, only behind Tulane and LSU-Baton Rouge.

Though interested that LSU-Shreveport had fared reasonably well in the rankings, I need not vacillate on what I think of the Gourman approach to quality assurance and assessment. A rating system that will let us compare the undergraduate quality of Mills College, the U.S. Air Force Academy, and Bemidji State University, to say nothing of the diverse institutions in Louisiana, is an instrument of some moment. Such ratings are educationally empty because they carry no significant meaning for students or public. To compare on a single scale, and to the accuracy of two decimal places, the quality of institutions of such diverse mission, admissions policy, program profile, community environment, student clientele, financial profile, and governance structure is educational mischief of the first order. The wonder is that Professor Gourman gets paid to do this, and that libraries will purchase his book.

At the time I received the phone calls, I had not yet seen the Gourman report. When I finally got my hands on the book, my judgments were only sharpened. Several prefaces are filled with puffed up rhetoric on the importance of the Gourman rankings and the inadequacies of voluntary accreditation. Nowhere in the report are we shown precisely what data were gathered, by what means, on what date. Nor are we told precisely who rendered judgments on the institutional data. For a thorough and informative analysis of the imperfections in the Gourman rankings, see David Webster's article, "Who Is Jack Gourman and Why Is He Saying All Those Things About My College" in the November/December 1984 issue of *Change*.

My point here, however, is to demonstrate that while we are busy debating the philosophical and technical difficulties of quality assurance, there are quality assurance challenges that require neither an elegant philosophy nor an imposing technology. They require only caring and courage.

The Quality Assurance Offensive

Let's examine illustrations of institutions already on the quality assurance offensive and see what benefits have accrued from those efforts.

Northeast Missouri State University over the last decade has implemented a "Value Added" quality assurance program that might be the envy of any institution. The university has assembled a comprehensive and useful array of data on its entering students (ACT scores and career interests). On this point, the university can claim little distinction. What is distinctive, however, is the comprehensive student data profile available from exit scores on the ACT COMP battery and from scores on nationally developed and locally developed instruments designed to assess knowledge and skill growth in various major fields. Feedback from questionnaires provides yet another dimension of information on the university's graduates. The most important outcome of this quality assurance effort is the application of the data for instructional improvement.

Here is an institution willing to act on the possible without waiting for the perfect assessment model. Northeast Missouri State University was awarded the prestigious Mitau Award by the American Association of State Colleges and Universities in 1983 for its effort.

The Tennessee Performance Funding Project is a quality assurance effort involving an entire state. Anticipating both public and professional concern with funding policies based on enrollment and with increased interest in accountability, the Tennessee Higher Education Commission (THEC), a state-level coordinating agency, implemented in the fall of 1974 a five-year, half-million dollar development effort called the Performance Funding Project. Its purpose was to explore the feasibility of allocating some portion of state funds on a performance criterion rather than solely on an enrollment criterion (Bogue and Brown 1982).

In the fall of 1979 a performance funding policy was implemented for the 1980-81 appropriations cycle. The policy permitted a college or university to earn an additional amount — up to 2% of its budget — based on its performance on the following five instructional variables:

1. Number of academic programs accredited, (for example, law, engineering, education, and business).
2. Performance of graduates on outcomes in general education (for example, ability to communicate, analyze, and evaluate, and familiarity with major modes of intellectual inquiry).
3. Performance of graduates on tests in their major fields (for example, nursing exams or engineering exams).
4. Evaluation of programs and services by enrolled students, recent alumni, and community-employer representatives, principally through follow-up questionnaires.
5. Peer evaluation of institutional programs by colleagues from similar institutions.

An institution could earn a maximum of 20 points on each variable, or up to a total of 100 points. Exhibit 1 illustrates one variable, performance outcomes in general education. *Note that these performance standards do not require that all colleges and universities adhere to the same definition of general education, nor do they require use of a common measure or indicator of performance.* For example, one university may require a mastery of basic economic concepts for all bachelor degree recipients, while another requires mastery of at least one computer language. Two colleges may both insist that students demonstrate proficiency in written communication but elect different measures of this proficiency. This protection of diversity generally holds for the other four variables as well.

Exhibit 1. Standards for Outcomes in General Education

1. The institution has assessed the performance of a representative sampling of graduates for its major degree — associate or bachelor's — on a measure of general education outcomes at least once during the past four years.

2. The institution has, during the last four years, assessed the general education performance of a representative sampling of its graduates by major field or college and has begun a program of interfield or intercollegiate analyses of the data.

3. The institution has an ongoing program to assess the performance of its graduates on a measure of general education outcomes and has available data, preferably on the same measure, for representative samples of two or more classes of graduates during the previous four years.

4. The institution meets the requirement of standard 3 and can further demonstrate for the most recent assessments that the development of its graduates — that is, the change in performance from freshman to graduation — is equivalent to or greater than the development of students for at least one institution whose freshman performance is on a comparable level.

General education outcomes are broadly defined as the knowledge and skills expected of graduates holding the same level of academic degree (for example, the bachelor's degree). Examples might include communication and problem-solving skills and familiarity with major modes of intellectual inquiry. The definition and selection of measurement instruments are left to individual institutions.

The standards are progressive in stringency and difficulty; for instance, the third is tougher than the second. Each subsumes the one before it, that is, the third standard cannot be attained without first attaining the second. Each standard in this category is worth 5 points for a maximum of 20.

The allocations available based on this evaluation ranged from $30,000 at smaller institutions up to a $1,000,000 at the state's largest institution. For the 1985-86 formula projection in Tennessee, the percentage devoted to the performance funding policy has been raised from the initial 2% to 5%; so now the maximum amount available to the largest institution in the state, the University of Tennessee at Knoxville, is $3,000,000. See Exhibit 2 for an illustration of how the first year of performance funding policy implementation in 1979-80 worked for Tennessee Technological University.

Exhibit 2. Tennessee Technological University's Ratings from the Tennessee Performance Funding Project

Tennessee Technological University (TTU), with an enrollment of approximately 8,000, offers bachelor's and master's degrees in arts and sciences, business, education, and nursing and degrees through the doctorate in engineering. In 1979, TTU had a base budget recommendation of approximately $12.5 million based on Tennessee's enrollment funding formula. The maximum amount available to TTU on the performance funding policy would be 2% of this base amount, or about $250,000. TTU received the following evaluations and point allocations on each of the five variables:

Variables	Maximum Points	Allowed Points
Programs accredited	20	17
Outcomes in general education	20	20
Outcomes in specialty fields	20	5
Follow-up evaluations	20	20
Peer evaluations	20	5
Total	100	67

Added to the budget recommendation for TTU was 67% of the maximum $250,000 available, or approximately $165,000.

Adoption and implementation of this policy followed a five-year effort involving 11 different campus-based pilot efforts among Tennessee colleges and universities — three community colleges, five regional universities, two universities offering doctorates, and a university health center. These campus-based projects were developed through performance contracts between THEC and the institutions and their governing boards. With relatively modest support, the 11 participating institutions contracted over a two-year period (1978-1979) to develop instructional performance indicators and to acquire initial data on these indicators. These pilot projects formed the basis for the performance funding policy previously described. Funded by $500,000 in grants from the Kellogg Foundation, the Ford Foundation, the Fund for Improvement of Postsecondary Education, and one anonymous foundation, the project was guided by both national and state advisory panels.

No legislative act or administrative regulation initiated this project. No law or rule required 11 different campuses to engage in the difficult and sensitive business of performance assessment. No edict by the THEC compelled these campuses and their governing boards to cooperate. This was a partnership effort in a state whose colleges and universities were determined to stay on the quality assurance offensive.

Readers interested in a more detailed description of this effort are referred to the original project report (Bogue 1980) and the 1982 *Harvard Business Review* article by Bogue and Brown.

The University of Tennessee at Knoxville is a second example of a major university that has discovered the renewing benefits of quality assurance efforts. This particular institutional effort also emerged from the Tennessee Performance Funding Project. Trudy Banta describes the implementation of quality assurance at the University of Tennessee in a recent paper (1984). She quotes a letter from Peter Ewell of the National Center for Higher Education Management Systems, which describes what the university has done:

> What is notable about the assessment process at UTK is not simply the excellence of its measurement technology. Nor is it the fact that individual academic programs and services have been changed as a result of applying the results obtained through this technology. Rather it is the fact that the entire institution — top management, unit administrators, researchers, faculty, and students themselves — has been thoroughly involved in the process. (p. 28)

A point I have made throughout this book is that we need to see both the journey and the arrival of leadership. This quality assurance "arrival" of the University of Tennessee was built on a decade of leadership at the university. At first, the adventurers were few and the benefits uncertain. The current constructive quality assurance at the university is a tribute to leadership persistence and commitment. Similar leadership records can be found in other Tennessee colleges and universities.

Quality Assurance — The Renewing Outcomes

With artistic administration, quality assurance can be an instrument of both institutional and personal renewal. Here are some of the ways this renewal function can be realized through evaluation.

Discovering Purpose. It is awkward when program evaluation proceeds without a clear definition of purpose. However, it is precisely this awkwardness that can often prove useful. As faculty undertake evaluation of programs, they often discover that their efforts are impeded because programs lack clarity of purpose. This, in turn, leads to an in-depth consideration of both goals and objectives, a worthwhile exercise.

Defining Priorities. When Robert Hutchins took over the presidency of the University of Chicago, he found that:

> The Great Depression conferred marked benefits upon the university, for it forced a reconsideration of the whole enterprise. The first thing I had to contend with was the demand that I cut everything 25 percent. This made no sense to me. I thought what was important should be supported and what was trivial should be dropped. (1968, p. 182)

Across-the-board cuts are often the first response to fiscal crisis. However, the kind of selective response described by Hutchins also is possible.

Facilitating Change. Faced with the possibility of a budget deficit of a half-million dollars if current programs and services were to be continued, a university executive officer recently called on his faculty and staff to evaluate all institutional programs and activities to see which might be revised or terminated to save operating funds. Likely targets included one or two professional programs with small student loads, high budgets, and in academic isolation from other programs. Another vulnerable activity was the institution's intercollegiate athletic program, which annually places a large drain on the operating budget. In this instance, evaluation facilitated change processes necessary for the institution's academic and fiscal health. Program evaluation can thus be a useful instrument for facilitating change. But such evaluations do not have to await fiscal crisis as the trigger mechanism.

Enlarging Understandings of Quality. At one point in *A Man for All Seasons*, King Henry remarks to Sir Thomas More, "Your taste in music is excellent. It exactly coincides with my own." This line reflects one of the more common understandings of the word "quality" in American education — definition by peer opinion. However, quality may be defined by other factors — high costs, selectivity, bigness, growth, achievement, availability, and diversity. One of the virtues of evaluation is that it brings richer understanding of "quality" because faculty and staff begin to struggle with the philosophical and technical questions of evaluation:

Should a single measure of achievement or a measure of change be used?

Should a standardized measure or one locally developed be used?

Should an absolute or a comparative standard be used to judge results?

Soon faculty begin to appreciate more fully the variety of meaning associated with "quality." In a community of learning, this is a useful and positive outcome.

Extending Value Sensitivities. If our vision of quality can be expanded through evaluation, so can other sensitivities. Those who struggle seriously with evaluation in education settings eventually will confront the question of measurement and meaning. They will rediscover that many meaningful events and outcomes do not yield to measurement: the warm smile on the student's face who discovers a new solution to a math problem, the satisfying grin from the student who masters a difficult skill, the serendipitous happenings in intellectual advance, the display of courage from men and women with ideas in advance of their time. A ray of sunlight falling through an early morning mist will reveal something about light that cannot be found in the laws of refraction. An orchestra performing Brahm's first symphony brings an appreciation of music not found in the mathematics of musical intervals. A disease that is brought under control with both minds and medicine at work brings understandings not to be found in anatomy and physiology alone.

76

Promoting Personnel Development. The Tennessee Performance Funding Project previously described depended heavily on the leadership of the campus pilot project directors. These directors came from a variety of academic disciplines. Few of them had previous experience in program evaluation. One of the major outcomes of this statewide evaluation activity was the personal development of the project directors at each campus and of the many faculty working with them. They had an opportunity to step outside their own academic field and to engage in a new line of inquiry. They had opportunity to probe new literature.

Physicists learned about the Delphi Technique. Historians examined standardized instruments for assessing general education competencies. Accountants studied the Institutional Goals Inventory. Sociologists reviewed the jury approach to the evaluation of data. And they all struggled with the interpersonal and management-of-change questions that faced them on their home campuses. Evaluation can thus present an opportunity for faculty and staff to explore new conceptual frontiers, to challenge their own educational biases, and to discover the excitement of placing ideas in action.

Quality Assurance Principles

There are good reasons for education leaders to be careful, even cautious, in quality assurance efforts. However, there are better reasons for leadership to reach beyond that caution, to discover the informing power of action. And there are good examples of the renewing benefits that can accrue to those who are willing to link reflection and action, to persevere beyond that first peak of resistance so that colleagues can discover the renewing benefits.

Some quality assurance opportunities are really very simple. A college vice president friend tells me of a 28-year-old student who brought a complaint to his office. This Vietnam veteran had been enrolled in an evening sophomore economics course in which the instructor gave only two tests, returned neither to the students, and never informed students of their status until final grades were issued by the registrar's office.

Following notification of his "D" grade and being placed on academic probation as a result of the grade in that one course, this student took time from his job for an 11:00 a.m. appointment to review his exams with the instructor. When the student arrived, the instructor kept the student waiting 15 minutes while he finished morning coffee with office colleagues, then told the student he could not find either of the student's exams. The student appealed to the department chairman and then to the dean, neither of whom found the student's complaint about the instructor's behavior worthy of pursuing. Thus the student's complaint to the vice president.

Entering where some academic administrators fear to tread, the vice president summoned all three colleagues to his office to ask what distorted sense

of ethics had led to this display of arrogance. The behavior of the offending instructor was at some variance with the glowing comments found on
the chairman's and dean's recommendation for the instructor's promotion
to assistant professor, which at that moment lay on the vice president's desk.
The vice president's pending review and action on the promotion request
suddenly enlivened each party's interest in the welfare of the student.

A new college dean friend tells me that he did not have to resort to an
elaborate evaluation to determine if the quality of his accounting department could be measured. What he has found is this:

- That only one of the last 25 graduates had passed the CPA exam.
- That the department's graduates have the worst CPA record in the
  state and that they have not moved from the cellar position in six years.
- That a recent visiting American Assembly of Collegiate Schools of
  Business team ranked the department the lowest in the college.
- That a recent self-study questionnaire of currently enrolled students
  revealed that the accounting department was accorded the lowest ratings of all departments in the college.
- That the dean's office has received seven letters of complaint during
  the last year from local accounting firm employers.
- That the department's graduates have scored the lowest of any department in the university on the ACT College Outcome Measures battery routinely administered by the university.

The barriers to quality assurance in these two cases are neither philosophical nor technical; they are simply cases of a lack of caring or a lack of
courage.

As I look back over this chapter, there are six principles that appear
promising to guide leaders in providing quality assurance.

1. *Effectiveness.* I prefer the term "effectiveness" to either "quality" or
   "excellence" because I think it simplifies and sharpens the issue. In
   determining effectiveness, we are simply answering the question of
   whether we have done what we intended to do in our educational
   programs and practices.
2. *Multiple Indicators.* There is no single indicator of educational performance that cannot be criticized for some theoretical or practical
   weakness. Therefore, an effective quality assurance program should
   provide feedback on several indicators of student performance (for
   example, change in student knowledge and skills, outcome performance measured against both criterion- and norm-referenced standards,
   student comments, etc.). In other words, we should depend not on
   one item of evidence but on a cluster of evidences.
3. *Student Impact.* It is surprising how many quality assurance efforts
   do not include any evidence on what students have learned or what

they think about their educational experience; therefore, I choose to give this principle special visibility. I am unable to conceive of any useful quality assurance effort that does not include some evidence on student impact — what students have learned and what their perceptions are for improvement of the educational experience.

4. *Performance Improvement.* The only valid reason for performance assessment is to obtain information that will help us do a better job. Performance improvement rather than punishment should thus be the guiding principle of evaluation.

5. *Mission Definition.* The environmental settings and missions of schools and colleges differ. There should be room for diversity and variance in performance indicators but no toleration of shoddy expectations for any mission.

6. *Unobtrusiveness.* None of us likes to work in a climate characterized by continuous and heavy breathing over the shoulder. Effective evaluation and quality assurance should be a natural and continuous part of the educational process.

There is a substantive literature emerging on the themes of educational evaluation and organizational effectiveness. Among the better resources on the general theme of educational evaluation, especially for the administrator new to social and behavior science fields, are the books by Anderson and Ball (1978), Guba and Lincoln (1981), and Worthen (1973). Helpful works on higher education evaluation are those by Hodgkinson and others (1975), Dressel (1976), and Miller (1979). On the theme of organizational effectiveness, the books by Goodman (1977) and Zammuto (1982) will prove informative. In addition to these works, see also Astin (1980) and Pace (1971, 1976).

Quality assurance is an adventure of learning in a community of learning. In serious quality assurance efforts are found opportunities to wonder at the extraordinary riches of human talent, to experience humility in the face of our immense ignorance, to know the challenge that comes in reaching beyond reason, to experience the satisfaction of doing a good work when critics and cynics told us we should not try and that we would not succeed. These are renewing benefits worthy of cultivation in an educational community. But most of all, we will know the pleasure of discovering our impact on students and of finding ways to strengthen that influence.

Mediocrity is an enemy of leadership.

References

Abernathy, William J., et al. *Industrial Renaissance*. New York: Basic Books, 1983.

Anderson, Scarvia, and Ball, Samuel. *The Profession and Practice of Program Evaluation*. San Francisco: Jossey-Bass, 1978.

Ashworth, Kenneth H. "When You Hear Hoofbeats, Don't Think of Zebras." *State Education Leader* 3 (Spring 1983): 10.

Astin, Alexander W. "When Does a College Deserve to be Called High Quality?" In *Current Issues in Higher Education*. Washington: American Association for Higher Education, 1980.

Astin, Alexander W., and Solmon, Lewis. "Are Reputational Ratings Needed to Measure Quality?" *Change* (October 1981): 14-19.

Banta, Trudy. *The NCHEMS/Kellogg Student Outcome Project at the University of Tennessee: Final Report 1982-84*. Knoxville: University of Tennessee, 1984.

Bloom, Benjamin. *Evaluation to Improve Learning*. New York: McGraw-Hill, 1981.

Bogue, E. Grady. *Allocation of State Funds on a Performance Criterion: The Report of the Performance Funding Project*. Nashville: Tennessee Higher Education Commission, 1980.

Bogue, E. Grady. "Outcomes: An Issue of Caring and Daring." *State Education Leader* 3 (Spring 1984): 10.

Bogue, E. Grady, and Brown, Wayne. "Performance Incentives for State Colleges." *Harvard Business Review* (November-December 1982): 123-28.

Cronbach, Lee. *Designing Evaluations of Educational and Social Programs*. San Francisco: Jossey-Bass, 1982.

Dressel, Paul L. *Handbook of Academic Evaluation*. San Francisco: Jossey-Bass, 1976.

Enarson, Harold L. "University or Knowledge Factory." *Chronicle of Higher Education*, 18 June 1973, p. 16.

Gardner, Don E. "Five Evaluation Frameworks." *Journal of Higher Education*, (September-October 1977): 571-93.

Goodman, Paul S., et al. *New Perspectives on Organizational Effectiveness*. San Francisco: Jossey-Bass, 1977.

Gourman, Jack. *The Gourman Report*. Los Angeles: National Education Standards, 1983.

Guba, Egon G., and Lincoln, Yvonne S. *Effective Evaluation*. San Francisco: Jossey-Bass, 1981.

Hodgkinson, Harold, et al. *Improving and Assessing Performance: Evaluation in Higher Education*. Berkeley, Calif.: Center for Research and Development in Higher Education, 1975.

Hutchins, Robert M. "First Glimpses of a New World." In *What I Have Learned*. New York: Simon & Schuster, 1968.

Involvement in Learning. Final Report of the Study Group on the Conditions of Excellence in American Higher Education. Washington, D.C.: National Institute of Education, October 1984.

Marcus, Laurence R., et al. *The Path to Excellence: Quality Assurance in Higher Education*. Washington, D.C.: Association for Study of Higher Education, 1983.

Messick, S. "The Standard Problem: Meaning and Values in Measurement and Evaluation." *American Psychologist* 30 (1975): 955-66.

Miller, Richard I. *The Assessment of College Performance*. San Francisco: Jossey-Bass, 1979.

Naisbitt, John. *Megatrends: Ten New Directions Transforming Our Lives*. New York: Warner Books, 1982.

Pace, C. Robert. *Evaluating Higher Education*. Tuscon: Higher Education Program, University of Arizona, July 1976.

Pace, C. Robert. *Thoughts on Evaluation in Higher Education*. Iowa City: The American College Testing Program, 1971.

Pirsig, Robert N. *Zen and the Art of Motorcycle Maintenance*. New York: William Morrow and Company, 1974.

Scully, Malcolm. "National Concern Over Educational Quality Seen Spreading from Schools to Colleges." *Chronicle of Higher Education*, 12 September 1984, p. 1.

Stuart, Jesse. *To Teach, To Love*. Baltimore: Penguin Books, 1973.

Webster, David S. "Advantages and Disadvantages of Methods of Assessing Quality." *Change* (October 1981): 20-24.

Worthen, Blaine R., and Sanders, James R. *Educational Evaluation: Theory and Practice*. Belmont, Calif.: Wadsworth, 1973.

Zammuto, Raymond F. *Assessing Organizational Effectiveness*. Albany: State University of New York Press, 1982.

Chapter Six

The Flogging of Theagenes

Imitation cannot go above its model. The imitator dooms himself to hopeless mediocrity.

— Ralph Waldo Emerson
An Address

There will always be those who will do better than I and those who will not, and no other fact could be more irrelevant to life's meaning.

— Hugh Prather
Notes on Love and Courage

I begin with an ancient story. What turn of fate led historians to record the story of Theagenes, a Greek athlete of 500 B.C., remains a mystery; but the story reminds us that history is a human construction and not a dry collection of events devoid of the historian's emotions, interests, and values. That such a remote item of history could be found 2,500 years later in the modest library at my institution is one of those pleasant intellectual treasures that fuels my curiosity each time I cross the threshold of a library.

A citizen of Thasus, Theagenes was a formidable athlete who won more than 1,400 prizes in the games of those days. On his death, admirers erected a statue in his honor. Apparently out of jealousy, one of his detractors came each evening to flog the statue of Theagenes. The nightly flogging continued, according to the ancient chronicles, until one evening the statue of Theagenes avenged itself by falling on the flogger, killing him.

Here is an ancient story with modern import, the tragic story of one talent throwing itself against the achievement of another, unable and unwilling to find a more constructive outlet than the flogging of a cold and sterile marker. How many unfortunate colleagues have you and I seen flogging the statue of Theagenes — expending precious energy and talent attacking the personality, the performance of others.

My purposes in this chapter are to show how poverty stricken and narrow our leadership vision can be, how imitation is the enemy of the effective leader, how easily jealousy can become a destructive force. The embracing purpose, of course, is to foster a larger vision of our own leadership potential.

The Edge of Arrogance — A Vision of Self

My first concern about the poverty of leadership vision is one of those statues we are often found flogging: a stereotypic notion of the leadership personality. Recently, a friend was competing for the president's position at a public university. He was asked by a member of the campus search committee how tall he was. His response of 5 feet 10 inches drew a furrowed brow from this psychology Ph.D., who apparently was afflicted with the idea that some minimum height was essential for presidential leadership. Whatever his background, the posture of this committee member reflected a monumental prejudice and ignorance. Of the two, perhaps ignorance is the least excusable. A Ph.D. who is a stranger to his own literature, to the lessons of history and biography, is a formidable curiosity.

In Shreveport, the president of Centenary College is a man diminutive in height only. I can look down on his height but not on his leadership record. Just 70 miles away, the president of Northwestern State University, a professional boxer who holds a doctorate in art, can look down on my height. I can match neither his expertise in boxing nor my Centenary friend's poetry and preaching power. Two presidential colleagues — one a Welsh poet, a Methodist minister, and former British naval officer all rolled into one; the other a boxer known for his sculpture. My aberration is that I play the French horn. Passing over the fact that there is little demand for my musical services, let me use this point to share an illustration about the appearance of leadership.

In 1952 I played first French horn in the Blue Band at Dixie Music Camp held at Arkansas A&M College in Monticello, Arkansas. The director of the Blue Band, the camp's most advanced band, was an unforgettable personality. Scrubby Watson was a short, rotund fellow from Pine Bluff, Arkansas. He had two withered fingers from an overexposure to X-rays in the early history of that diagnostic tool. One glass eye had the disturbing habit of wandering around the rehearsal hall while the one good eye remained fixed on the music and musicians. At the grand finale concert, which ended each year with Sousa's "Stars and Stripes Forever," Scrubby would forsake all dignity on the podium by turning to the audience and imitating the technical flourishes of the piccolos by holding his baton to his mouth.

I had won the first chair in the Blue Band that year over the first chair of the Arkansas State Band. I thought I was pretty good. One day we were making our way through Wagner's "Siegfried's Rhine Journey." When we arrived at my solo part, I splattered bad notes all over the rehearsal hall. Not willing to let this sloppy performance pass, Scrubby stopped the band in mid-phrase, fixed the one good eye on me, and said: "Grady, you've been telling all the girls what a hotshot horn player you are, and here you are wandering around the music like a blind dog in a meat factory."

This was an intense moment of embarrassment in my young life, and I yearned to slither away. That week I took to the shade trees for practice and rendered a near-perfect solo at the Friday evening concert. I still remember the warm thrill of mastery and also the painful moment of discipline it took to produce it.

Scrubby Watson was a leader in my life. He enjoys a moment of immortality because his act of caring and correction lives on in my life. With that bad eye, those burned-off fingers, and that rotund physique, I wonder how many folks told Scrubby that he could never be a conductor. Would I have remembered Scrubby if he had been a dashing figure in black tails? Perhaps. But not with as much clarity or affection.

Leaders who agree with the theme of the opening chapter — that ignorance is the first enemy of leadership — will appreciate affirmation from some of the better leadership literature. From *The Human Dilemmas of Leadership* (1966) by Abraham Zaleznik comes this note:

> The exercise of leadership requires a strong sense of identity — knowing who one is and who one is not. The myth of the value of being an "all-around guy" is damaging to the striving of an individual to locate himself from within and then to place himself in relation to others. This active location and placement of oneself prevents the individual from being defined by others in uncongenial terms. It prevents him also from being buffeted around the sea of opinion he must live within. A sense of autonomy, separateness, or identity permits a freedom of action and thinking so necessary for leadership. (pp. 41-42)

From Peter Drucker's *The Effective Executive* (1966) comes this affirming note:

> Among the effective executives I have known and worked with, there are extroverts and aloof, retiring men, some even morbidly shy. Some are eccentrics; others painfully correct conformists. Some are fat and some are lean. Some are worriers, some are relaxed. Some drink quite heavily, others are total abstainers. Some are men of great charm and warmth, some have no more personality than a frozen mackerel. There are a few men among them who would answer to the popular conception of a "leader." But equally there are colorless men who would attract no attention in a crowd. Some are scholars and serious students, others almost unlettered. Some have broad interests, others know nothing except their own narrow area and care for little else. Some of the men are self-centered, if not indeed selfish. But there are also some who are generous of heart and mind. There are men who live only for their work, and others whose main interests lie outside — in the community work, in their church, in the study of Chinese poetry, or in modern music. Among the effective executives I have met, there are people who use logic and analysis and others who rely mainly on perception and intuition. There are men who make decisions easily and men who suffer agonies every time they have to move. (p.22)

And in James MacGregor Burns' *Leadership* (1978), we learn that:

> Eleanor Roosevelt's early years were a desperate period of desertion and loneliness. (p. 60)

> Even in his preschool years Gandhi seems to have had feelings of insecurity about his appearance — his sharp facial features, big ears, small frame — his physical prowess, and his manliness. (p. 55)

> Tommy [Thomas Woodrow Wilson] did not learn the written alphabet until he was nine, enter school until ten, or learn to read easily until eleven. . .like Gandhi, much earlier, did badly in studies and in sports. (p. 102)

From my limited biographical exposure, I found it fascinating, perhaps even reassuring, to learn that Gen. Douglas MacArthur loved western movies, that Andrew Jackson owed large sums of money most of his life, that John Wesley could know jealousy, that a retiring and skinny James Manchester could become a Marine Corps fighter, that Agatha Christie tried to have her husband framed for murder, that the renowned French sculptor Rodin failed to gain admission to the prestigious School of Arts, that Leon Uris does not have a college degree, that Harlan Sanders was 65 years old when he started Kentucky Fried Chicken.

What are we to conclude from this limited adventure into the leadership literature and in biography? Is it that a deprived childhood, big ears, and lack of sports interest may combine to produce a leader in latter years? No, I think the lesson to be learned is quite beautifully captured by Emerson in his essay on *Compensation*:

> As no man had ever a point of pride that was not injurous to him, so no man had ever a defect that was not somewhere made useful to him. Has he a defect of temper that unfits him to live in society? Thereby he is driven to entertain himself alone and acquire habits of self help; and thus, like the wounded oyster, he mends his shell with a pearl. (p. 161)

There are no leaders without personality frailty or imperfection. A will to action marks the leader, a willingness to enter the field of human interaction where we learn that pain is the mother of compassion, that correction is the author of wisdom, that daring sharpens decision, that courage enobles the spirit, that in seeds of doubt reside the flowers of faith.

I worry about expectations that wear away the beautiful edges of personality, working to make us smooth little pebbles that will rub against each other without much friction. When everything in our experience affirms the power of personality diversity, why are we so intent in wearing down those differences? What strength of soul and spirit is required to develop and maintain some vision of self? Leaders know. Francis Bacon knew when years ago he wrote, "It is a sad fate for a man to die too well known to others, and still unknown to himself."

Is it possible that the edge of arrogance may be required to fortify leader personality against an inevitable assault of cynicism and criticism? How will leaders distinguish the advice of busy little critics, who carry their black clouds of pessimism and suspicion, from the well-intentioned counsel of honest but dissenting loyalty? Under what circumstances shall we adjust or compromise? And when is the moment that we must stand in lonely isolation, rejecting even well-intentioned counsel that we judge to be in error?

Perhaps it is not the edge of arrogance that is required but simply a quiet confidence, a confidence earned through taking risks in previous decisions. Thus, through success and failure, the leader learns a little more about his strengths and limitations. One remains a leader only by being willing to take risks in ventures that may result in both satisfying and painful outcomes.

The Centipede Syndrome — A Vision of Style

Having challenged the conventional wisdom of how one gets to be a leader, whether by personality or pedigree, I now will take on those who are flogging the statue of leadership style — how one behaves as a leader.

There have been a number of recent books on presidential style and leadership in higher education. In one of the more recent books, *Power of the Presidency* (1984), former college president and now president of the Council for the Advancement and Support of Education (CASE), James Fisher emphasizes the charismatic power in the presidency. He concludes that the major components of charisma are distance, style, and perceived self-confidence. Suggesting that a certain mystery should surround the president, Fisher ends his opening chapter with this terse line of counsel: "Never, never get off that presidential platform" (p. 12).

I was in my fifth year as chancellor when I read Fisher's book. I couldn't help but wonder whether I had created sufficient mystery and distance in my relationships with colleagues and faculty. What did it portend for my leadership effectiveness if some of my colleagues referred to me as Grady rather than Dr. Bogue or Chancellor? Should I rearrange the staff conference table so that the vice chancellors were seated at some respectful distance. Perhaps I should wear my academic regalia to staff meetings.

I was just getting into this matter of charismatic style when I glanced over to my bookshelves and recalled other books on the presidency. Victor Baldridge and associates offered a political model of the presidency in *Policy Making and Effective Leadership* (1978); and Donald Walker emphasized the need for the informed presidency in his splendid book, *The Effective Administrator*. Warren Bennis revealed the vulnerable presidency in *The Unconscious Conspiracy* (1976). Joseph Kauffman offered us a view of the servant president in *At the Pleasure of the Board* (1980). Michael Cohen and James March revealed the impotent president in *Leadership and Ambiguity* (1974).

Without realizing it, I began to suffer the symptoms of that dreaded disease, the "centipede syndrome." I began to think so much about style that I didn't know which foot to put down next. From somewhere in the recesses of my memory, however, came forth that response of Ella Fitzgerald when she was asked if she ever wondered about her identity. To which Miss Fitzgerald responded: "Honey, I didn't worry about identity. I just was."

A brief conceptual diversion may be helpful here. The concept of leadership and management style has its origins in research appearing in major publications in the Fifties and Sixties. The research, when distilled, concludes with this common finding — that leadership behavior can be factored into two independent variables: a task-orientation variable and a person-oriented variable. There followed from the research a number of style assessment instruments to assist leaders or managers in assessing their basic style inclination. Gradually there began to evolve among practicing managers the conviction that there was some ideal style.

Canadian author W.J. Reddin put this notion to rest, however, with a splendid book, *Managerial Effectiveness* (1970), in which he added a third dimension — an effectiveness dimension — to the two previous factors of task and personal relationships. Reddin rejected the idea that there was an ideal managerial style. Nevertheless, the interest in style continues, especially in college and university management, as can be seen in the recent publication *The Academic Administrator Grid: A Guide to Developing Effective Management Teams* (Blake et al. 1981).

A recent and fairly simple guide to understanding the relationships between leader behavior and follower behavior can be found in Paul Hersey's *The Situational Leader* (1984). He provides a descriptive guide to leadership styles and a prescriptive model for matching leadership style with the readiness of followers.

Leaders can profit from the technical literature I have mentioned. The concepts, the illustrations, the value dispositions, the experience, and the research of practitioners and scholars are all eminently worthy of our study and reflection. But they can be harmful if we succumb to shallow imitation of the style advice offered. I know administrators with a blood-and-guts style, a few who manage well with the Godfather style, a few more who fit well in the patriarchal style, and one or two that approximate a Lt. Fuzz style in the "Beetle Bailey" comic strip. The interaction of their styles with their personality and leadership settings is what makes them highly effective. And effective ones will spend no time worrying where they fit in my taxonomy of leadership styles.

This venture into questions of leadership style and into the sources of our knowledge and belief about style brings me to this closing note. Education institutions are a precious enterprise, an enterprise devoted to the nurture of leadership in many fields. Those of us who carry leadership responsibility for this enterprise often perpetuate a view of leadership heavily centered on matters practical and political, economic and utilitarian. James Kavanaugh's poem below reminds me that we live in a world of multiple realities, of fact and feeling, and that we must prepare leaders for both of these worlds.

There Are Men Too Gentle to Live Among Wolves

There are men too gentle to live among wolves
    Who prey upon them with IBM eyes
And sell their hearts and guts for martinis at noon
    There are men too gentle for a savage world
Who dream instead of snow and children and Halloween
    And wonder if the leaves will change their color soon.

There are men too gentle to live among the wolves
    Who annoint them for burial with greedy claws
And murder them for a merchant's profit and gain
    There are men too gentle for a corporate world
Who dream instead of candied apples and ferris wheels
    And pause to hear the distant whistle of a train.

There are men too gentle to live among wolves
    Who devour them with eager appetite and search
For other men to prey upon and suck their childhood dry.
    There are men too gentle for an accountant's world
Who dream instead of Easter eggs and fragrant grass
    And search for beauty and mystery of the sky.

There are men too gentle to live among wolves
    Who toss them like a lost and wounded dove.
Such gentle men are lonely in a merchant's world
    Unless they have a gentle one to love. (1970)

Choosing Motives to Live By —
A Vision of Performance Standards

My final lesson from the flogging of Theagenes is probably the most damaging of all. It has to do with the motives we use to judge others' performance compared to our own. Let me illustrate with a personal anecdote.

It is my habit early in the morning to take my collie, Coco, for a brisk walk of about two miles. Three or four days a week I return and jump on my 10-speed Sears bike for additional aerobic exercise around the neighborhood. Keep in mind, now, that I am no sophisticated cyclist. I wear no helmet; and anyone who rides a Sears bike can hardly be described as a serious cycling athlete.

One morning I encountered a fellow cyclist who passed me going in the opposite direction. He wore a pair of khaki cutoffs, a T-shirt, black socks, John Deere cap, and a pair of beat-up white Keds. He appeared to be in command of his 1953 balloon-tired Schwinn. We exchanged friendly greetings and continued on our respective tours around the neighborhood. Watching him cycle reminded me of the fellow who made me give up golf back in the early 1960s, the fellow who played the Overton Park golf course in Memphis with only a 3-iron for driving, chipping, and putting – and beat my score by 20 points.

Sure enough, on the next pass around the subdivision I noticed that the cyclist had advanced on me by a block or so. My competitive instinct took over. Perhaps if I took Tampa Street at the end of the subdivision, I could cut my usual route by a quarter of a mile, and this would allow me to show him up on the next pass. The devil was sitting on my shoulder as I considered this alternative. The angels intervened, however, suggesting that I was about to prostitute the purpose of my early morning ride. I resisted the temptation and proceeded on the regular course. But the "Great Deluder" was still at work: I was conscious of pressing the pedals with a little more vigor so that when I next passed my friend we would be about even.

After six trips around the subdivision, I decided that an early morning ride of 14 miles or so was healthy enough and I pulled into the house to take my shower and shave. Some 45 minutes later, refreshed and renewed, I came out of my house, got into my car, and started off to work. Who should pass but my new friend in the khaki cutoffs, smiling and waving. This fellow had doubled my time and distance! The cruelest cut of all was that he appeared not even to be sweating. I bet he plays golf with a 3-iron, too.

Here are the choices I faced regarding my performance standards:

1. *Absolute versus relative.* Would I ride to an expectation I had previously set or to the standard set by my early morning friend? What effect would his performance have on me tomorrow?

2. *Substantive versus pseudo.* Would I evaluate my biking friend on appearance? He was not dressed in the regalia of a power cyclist, but he certainly had power.

3. *Short-term versus long-term.* Would I sacrifice the future to make today's ride look a little better? In whose eyes?

4. *Achievable versus ideal.* Would I cycle for a standard that was certain to yield immediate satisfaction or set some ideal standard as a challenge?

5. *Quantitative versus qualitative.* Would I ride to the criterion of distance or time or for the private pleasure of that early morning sunrise?

6. *Personal versus public standards.* Would I adjust my standard of performance in the face of perceived competition?

These questions of performance standards are trivial when one is dealing with an early morning bike ride but not so trivial when we cross the threshold of our office doors each morning. We cannot make meanings for others until we have first found meaning for ourselves. That meaning is operationally expressed in our standards of performance and success.

In a special place in my personal library are three volumes that rest on a shelf just below a row of books on management and leadership. The three are novels: *Les Miserables* by Victor Hugo, *The Citadel* by A.J. Cronin, and *Cry, The Beloved Country* by Alan Paton. In a way these are excellent texts on management and leadership. They are fictional, yet powerful, accounts of men choosing motives to live by. Of Javert and Jean Valjean choosing mercy and justice, of Dr. Andrew Manson and Dr. Freddie Hampton choosing service and profit, of Stephen Kumalo and James Jarvis choosing love over revenge.

We also choose. We can choose to flog the statue of some Theagenes or we can choose motives that direct our lives toward more noble visions. These motives become operational when we are willing:

To critically evaluate conventional wisdom,

To search for alternatives when conventional channels close off our aspirations for improvement,

To take action and make decisions when reason offers no certain path,

To persist in the face of failure,

To welcome ambiguity in personal relationships,

To accent performance rather than pedigree,

To both accept and reject criticism,

To know fear and hurt but keep on going.

When we are willing to trust ourselves while inner doubts assail our outer confidence, then we will have the capacity to provide inspiration and meaning for others. Then we will stop the flogging of Theagenes and begin to erect the only worthy monument to leadership − the investment of our talent in the service of noble principle and the nurture of the talent and potential of those who look to us for inspiration.

Postscript

Why is it that some blame their own lack of accomplishment on the success of others' achievements? Why do we lack the ability to rejoice at another's achievement? Why do we believe that showing pleasure at the achievement or success of others might make us look less competitive, less aggressive? I hope that this chapter has provided answers to these questions.

My theme in this chapter has been neither complex nor profound. Wherever our heart and interest may lie − whether in poetry or politics, music or management, literature or law — we will never know the true potential of leadership by throwing our talent, our lives, our energy against the style, the standards, the successes of another. There is, in a word, no elevating effect to be derived from putting others down.

Finally this. Imitation is a cheap and shallow path to leadership. Imitation never allows us to plumb the depths of our own potential, to know our own strength and frailty. And without that self-knowledge there can be no leadership of others.

Imitation is an enemy of leadership.

References

Baldridge, J. Victor, et al. *Policy Making and Effective Leadership*. San Francisco: Jossey-Bass, 1978.

Bennis, Warren. *The Unconscious Conspiracy: Why Leaders Can't Lead*. New York: AMACOM, 1976.

Blake, Robert R., et al. *The Academic Administrator Grid: A Guide to Developing Effective Management Teams*. San Francisco: Jossey-Bass, 1981.

Blake, Robert R., and Mouton, Jane Srygly. *The Managerial Grid*. Houston: Gulf, 1964.

Bogue, E.G., and Saunders, Robert L. *The Educational Manager: Artist and Practitioner*. Worthington, Ohio: Charles A. Jones, 1976.

Burns, James MacGregor. *Leadership*. New York: Harper & Row, 1978.

Chickering, Arthur W. *Education and Identity*. San Francisco: Jossey-Bass, 1971.

Cohen, Michael D., and March, James G. *Leadership and Ambiguity: The American College President*. New York: McGraw-Hill, 1974.

Cronin, A.J. *The Citadel*. Boston: Little, Brown and Company, 1937,

Drucker, Peter F. *The Effective Executive*. New York: Harper & Row, 1966.

Emerson, Ralph Waldo. "An Address." In *The Portable Emerson*, edited by Mark Van Doren. New York: Viking Press, 1969.

Emerson, Ralph Waldo. "Compensation." In *The Complete Writings of Ralph Waldo Emerson*. Vol. I. New York: William H. Morrow, 1929.

Fiedler, Fred E. *A Theory of Leadership Effectiveness*. New York: McGraw-Hill, 1967.

Fisher, James L. *Power of the Presidency*. New York: American Council on Education, Macmillan, 1984.

Getzels, Jacob W., et al. *Educational Administration as a Social Process*. New York: Harper & Row, 1968.

Hersey, Paul. *The Situational Leader*. New York: Warner Books, 1984.

Hugo, Victor. *Les Miserables*. New York: Simon & Schuster, 1964.

Kauffman, Joseph F. *At the Pleasure of the Board: The Service of the College and University President*. Washington: American Council on Education, 1980.

Kavanaugh, James. *There Are Men Too Gentle to Live Among Wolves*. Los Angeles: Nash, 1970.

Paton, Alan. *Cry, The Beloved Country*. New York: Scribner's, 1948.

Prather, Hugh. *Notes on Love and Courage*. New York: Doubleday, 1977.

Reddin, William J. *Managerial Effectiveness*. New York: McGraw-Hill, 1970.

Shartle, Carroll Leonard. *Executive Performance and Leadership*. Englewood Cliffs, N.J.: Prentice-Hall, 1956.

Walker, Donald E. *The Effective Administrator*. San Francisco: Jossey-Bass, 1979.

Zaleznik, Abraham. *The Human Dilemmas of Leadership*. New York: Harper & Row, 1966.

Chapter Seven

The Other Half of Wisdom

Men who boast of being what is called "practical" are for the most part exclusively preoccupied with means. But theirs is only one half of wisdom. When we take account of the other half, which is concerned with ends, the economic process and the whole of human life take on an entirely new aspect. We ask no longer: What have the producers produced, and what has consumption enabled the consumers in their turn to produce? We ask instead: What has there been in the lives of the consumers and producers to make them glad to be alive?

— Bertrand Russell
Authority and the Individual

A Man who becomes conscious of the responsibility he bears toward a human being who affectionately awaits him, or to an unfinished work, will never be able to throw away his life. He knows the "why" for his existence, and will be able to bear almost any "how."

— Victor Frankl
Man's Search for Meaning

American colleges and universities are servant organizations. American higher education has been involved in strengthening the cultural, social, and economic health of our nation from the inception of the Land Grant concept in the latter part of the nineteenth century. This role, described by Boyer and Hechinger in their concise and constructive book *Higher Learning in the Nation's Service* (1981), is unique to American colleges and universities.

However, there is a risk in that role, which Boyer and Hechinger describe as follows:

While responding to the national agenda, higher learning, at its best, also acts as conscience and critic of society, thus risking the displeasure of the established order. To some, the two strands of that tradition – the academy as both servant and critic of society – may seem violently contradictory. We, however, are convinced that both strands are equally essential. Taken together they form a remarkable record of service to the nation. (p. 20)

There is a grand record in the service role of our colleges and universities. However, there are several faces to the servant role of colleges and universities. A few vignettes serve to tell another story about the extent to which we are servant institutions and provide us with further insights into our leadership roles.

The Servant University – Snarls and Smiles

A 30-year-old woman interested in furthering her education leaves her job as a secretary at the city utility company at 4:30 p.m. and fights the cross-town traffic to reach the university registrar's office before 5:00. She reaches the registrar's door at 5:01, and a service sourpuss suggests that she come back in the morning at 8:00. No community goodwill earned here. Not only is service not available at lunch time or in the evenings or weekends, it comes packaged in grim faces when the registrar office doors are open. Where is leadership hiding?

A 40-year-old attorney enrolls to take a course in BASIC as a means of becoming more proficient on his new personal computer at the office. Illness in his family causes him to withdraw after only one class meeting. The business office, which insisted on cash payment for his tuition at the day of registration, takes six weeks to furnish a refund and then, according to this institution's policy, the student receives only a 50% refund. Unlike Sears, where refunds are issued on the spot with a smile in exchange for continuing customer loyalty, at this university the loyalty and feelings of the student have yet to be considered.

An 18-year-old aspiring student makes an appointment to visit with the financial aid officer of the local community college. He arrives on time with his divorced mother, a woman who completed only six years of grade school but is eager to explore every way for her son to attend college. A surly financial aid officer tells them to go to the admissions office and file an application to indicate seriousness in attending this institution before he will talk further with them. How long will it take a good faculty and other able administrative colleagues to compensate for this unfortunate act of ill will?

An aspiring young journalist looks forward to taking an introductory philosophy course as a means of intellectual enrichment and renewal. She arrives at the first class meeting and takes her place with other bright faces, plus a few anxious ones. The instructor enters, and the class is treated to a full blast of professorial pomposity. They are told how many can expect to fail the course, that no excuses are accepted for absences, that only one exam will be given, and that the exam will determine the grade in the course. Following this chilling introduction, the professor proceeds to lecture the class with a dull and belabored reading from the text. How many inspiring and exciting classrooms will it take to counteract this professor's behavior, and where is departmental leadership here?

In addition to the "public face" colleges and universities present, there are the service snafus that occur within the institution: buildings and grounds cluttered with trash because neither students nor grounds crew care, faculty members carrying a smoldering anger because of rude treatment in the campus bookstore, accounting clerks mad at the faculty because a callous faculty member just treated them to a verbal assault. Attitudes of service are a community concern. The reputation of the schools in a community are earned by a thousand small acts of courtesy, a helping hand, a smiling face, a knowledgeable response, an empathic heart.

Attending a Chamber of Commerce dinner one evening, I braced myself when the president of the organization asked me to see him after the dinner on a matter related to the university. I was relieved when he described how a member of the faculty had assisted his wife, who was confused by the spring registration procedures. He took the trouble to walk with her through the entire registration process. I went back to campus the next morning and wrote a personal thank you to that man who put a smiling face on the university.

Recently I went with one of our English professors to a retirement home and watched the pleasure and warmth he brought to the smiling and eager faces of students ranging in age from 65 to 95. Here is a servant professor who communicates to his students that learning can take place until the lights go out, who kindles anew the flame of learning in these still active minds. His pay for doing this civic service is a pittance. He struggles each year to find financial support for a work that is not easy to sell. He understands firsthand the truth of Gilbert Highet's observation that:

> Lawyers and doctors are engaged in preserving men's and women's lives and property; while teachers and clergymen do but help furnish their minds and souls . . . men will pay more to be delivered from danger than to be assisted in developing themselves. (p. 55)

It is winter in Shreveport. We have just been treated to a white surprise, a four-inch snow that would hardly be worth a yawn in Chicago or Buffalo. For panicky drivers in the Deep South, however, this is a wild time on the city streets. It takes me four hours to travel the five miles from a downtown luncheon meeting to the campus. We close the university for an afternoon and a day.

On the day we reopen, one of our students presents himself unannounced in my office. I recognize him as one of our majors in the arts. I invite him in for a cup of hot chocolate and brace myself for a complaint. He has come to tell me how much he appreciated the thoughtful act of one of our student affairs administrators, who picked him up on the highway in front of our snow-blanketed deserted campus when the city buses failed to make their schedules. This administrator carried the student four miles to his home, taking some three hours to navigate a mad melee of cars littering the streets and ditches. What a nice way to start the morning. This is a smiling face of service. I walk over to the administrator's office to say how much I appreciate this act of kindness and how contagious it will be.

The 1984 annual report for Louisiana State University in Shreveport uses the theme of "Servant University" to show our involvement in the civic life of our community. Here are some snapshots of this involvement:

A professor of history helping to prune the city rose beds,

A professor of economics helping with a free meal program in a deprived area of the city,

A professor of education and a professor of management helping with the United Way Campaign,

An administrator, a professor, and a class helping with the Scouts public relations campaign,

An administrator helping with the search committee for a new symphony conductor,

A professor of physical education helping with a Special Olympics program on campus,

A professor of sociology conducting a survey of needs in a deprived housing area,

A professor of mathematics teaching a special computer course for talented high school students and an inservice program for teachers,

A professor of education teaching in a home for runaways,

A professor of biology working as a judge in regional and national science fairs,

A professor of history serving on a special mayoral committee on the status of women,

A student affairs officer helping organize and implement a career day for high school students and area businesses.

A hundred other faces of service are carried to almost every civic and professional board in the urban area. Countless quiet acts of service are carried out in the homes of our faculty and staff. Most of these acts do not make the papers, but they nevertheless make quiet news across our community.

The ideal of service can be corrupted by some types of leadership. I still carry the scars of an early interaction with a service grouch, a financial executive whose credentials and experience made him a knowledgeable man; but his pompous behavior was such that he had yet to engage the enemy of arrogance.

He had become a 200-pound accounting and auditing manual, a financial Scrooge who never met a man he couldn't tag with an audit exception, a sad and empty man whose mind had been replaced with a disk file of fiscal regulation, a hardened man obsessed by the belief that the real world was full of chicanery. His arrogance deprived him of the opportunity to use his considerable talent in more effective service.

It is not only educators whose arrogance leads them to adopt an imperious attitude unworthy of the servant leader. I have a friend who recently suffered a heart attack. Intelligent and interested in improving his health, he read seriously and extensively on nutrition, stress, and exercise. When he asked his cardiologist about the books he had read, the cardiologist asked how much my friend had spent for these books. When told that all were available in paperback and that the investment probably was not more than $18.95, the cardiologist responded that the advice and information in these books were worth about that amount. For this display of arrogance, my friend soon received a computer billing for $125.00 from his cardiologist.

Service and Accountability

Public confidence in the professions is lacking, and the likelihood of future tensions between laity and professional is high. This is tragic because both the servant and those served will lose in these transactions.

The litany of complaints is lengthy. Attorneys are chided for masking simple matters in obscure jargon and for violating the law they are sworn to uphold. The clergy are accused of forsaking their role in advancing modern morality, leaving philosophers and humanists to lead contemporary movements for justice. Engineers are chastised for roofs that leak, windows that fall from skyscrapers, and engines that drop from planes. Accountants are pictured as master chefs, good at cooking the books. Businessmen want us to honor the profit motive as essential to the forward movement of society. The public mind understands, however, that the profit motive is not the only motive worthy of honor in our society. If it were, Michaelangelo would have been a comic strip illustrator, Descartes and Newton wholesalers for arithmetic puzzles, Emerson a bookbinder, Jonas

97

Salk a drugstore proprieter, and generals George Marshall and Douglas MacArthur manufacturers of toy soldiers.

One could argue that, like the poor, the errant professional is always with us. However, just one such errant professional is too many — just one teacher who fears to love his or her students by expecting the best of them, just one physician whose view is so colored by arrogance and affluence that patients are seen as objects with a dollar sign affixed, just one attorney who has forsaken the principle of justice for a life of duplicity and deceit, just one who has grown so accustomed to looking down on the people that he has forgotten what beauty there is in looking up to them. Just one is too many! There is no place for arrogance in effective leadership.

The Servant Leader — A Maker of Meaning

In my home library is a small volume of only 142 pages. It is Victor Frankl's *Man's Search for Meaning*. Frankl reports that amid the horror of German prisoner of war camps, which he experienced firsthand as a captive physician, he saw men survive every conceivable torture of body and spirit because they had a will to live, a hope for the future. But he saw others who had no obvious organic reasons to die, but lacking hope and meaning in their lives, curl up in the fetal position and give up life. Frankl concludes that "Man's search for meaning is a primary force in his life and not a 'secondary rationalization' of instinctual drives" (p. 99).

Servant leaders have found meaning in their lives, and they communicate that meaning to those whose lives they touch. The leader who inspires an attitude of service in his colleagues is a maker of meaning. But for some the vision of meaning is a limited one.

For many leaders growth is an end in itself. The measure of their achievement, their vision of meaning, is to be found in a growth chart with a positive slope — increased enrollments, larger budgets, more faculty, additional buildings. Such growth leads them to write bold lines in their annual reports, but such writings are often on perishable bond. When enrollments go down, the football team has a losing season, or a building named for a former president is torn down for a parking lot, the potential for trauma is high.

For other leaders there is the seductive call of public approbation. Who among us can ignore this powerful need in our lives — the need for approval, affection, affirmation. We all need the reinforcement that comes from knowing that our actions and decisions are accepted, endorsed, welcomed. The danger lies in the need for constant consensus as a mark of leadership achievement.

A vice president friend told me that, following an unpopular decision on his part, he was chastised by one of his new deans. This new dean had criticized the vice president for failing to acknowledge the collegial model of consensus in the decision-making process. This young dean had yet to encounter one of those heart-wrenching ethical decisions that pit the loneliness of doing what is right against the might of popular opinion. The servant leader is filled with care and kindness, but not with weakness.

For a few leaders the performance measure is mobility, the speed with which they climb the executive ladder, the number of stars worn on their academic epaulets. For some education leaders mobility is an appropriate and legitimate testimony to their talent and courage. For others it is nothing more than selfish ambition, leaving in its wake the bent backs of men and women who served as rungs on the ladder.

Then there are those leaders who measure their performance by the volume of their activity. They carry heavy vitas listing frequent but surface involvements, many of which came to them not because of ability but because of position. For them, leadership is not so much achievement and ability as visibility. Granted, the sensitive application of social intelligence as to where we seen and with whom is important; but when such efforts at visibility are a thin veneer representing convention rather than conviction, the displacement of means and ends is too obvious to ignore.

And finally, there is the leader who rejoices in power. It would be difficult to find a contemporary book on management, and college management in particular, without finding the word "power" in title or index. I look over the carriage of my typewriter and see two titles in front of me. There is the relatively new book, *Power of the Presidency* (1984) by Fisher; and then there is an older volume, *Power, Presidents, and Professors* (1967) by Demerath and others. And in George Keller's 1983 publication, *Academic Strategy*, we find this note:

> There is now a stalemate in the exercise of power on the American campus. . . . At the very time that the need for strong leadership in higher education has reached new levels of urgency, academic management is in chains. Indeed, the whole subject of administration in higher education is befuddled and bound by rusty myths and hoary notions about authority, management, and leadership. (p. 27)

The kinds of power available to the college president or any other administrator are neither new nor mysterious. There is the power of position, of competence, of personality, of character. Or if one prefers Fisher's taxonomy, there is coercive power, reward power, legitimate power, expert power, and charismatic power (Fisher 1984, pp. 27-42).

The servant leader is not a stranger to power. He simply realizes that power is an instrument awaiting the engagement of more important questions: For what end, for what purpose, for what meaning will power be employed? Growth, public approval, mobility, activity, power — all these can be appropriate indicators of leadership achievement. However, the servant leader keeps these indicators in balance and holds a more complete vision of leadership effectiveness. That vision provides a place for the indicators discussed below.

A Compassion for the Common Man. Returning from a trip to the state capital recently, I took advantage of a few private moments and cleared the busy pathways of my mind with moments of musical interlude from the car stereo. A rousing bit of musical Americana, Aaron Copeland's "Fanfare for the Common Man," is a bright and brassy salute to the quiet folks of history.

The common man — I see him everyday. Zurline and Irving keep the hallways clean and greet me with a smile each morning. Blackwell has worked in the maintenance department for 17 years. His daily devotion to the smooth functioning of steam valves and air conditioning compressors is a matter of critical interest only when they fail to function on an extremely hot or cold day. With a smile on his face and a wrench in his hand, he goes about his work with cheer and quiet competence. Hubert Humphreys is retiring this year after teaching history for many years at the university. I doubt that we will find a biography of Hubert in our library in the future; but the record of his devotion lives on in the hearts, minds, and souls of men and women for whom he cared.

There is a line in Will Durant's opening volume on *The Story of Civilization* that says, "virtuous men, like happy nations, have no history." But they really do have a history, though perhaps not a written one. There is a reality of goodness that is carried from one generation to the next by that great and beautiful mass of the common man, who struggle each day, living noble lives of quiet splendor.

Two decades ago I read a little book, *The Thunder of Bare Feet* by W.W. Hamilton. The theme of this book is that history is filled with the sounds of leather slippers and silk stockings going down the stairs and the thunder of bare feet coming up the stairs. The servant leader understands both the philosophical and practical import of having compassion for the barefoot man. He treats each person with dignity, looking for the spark of curiosity and creativity in every heart and soul, knowing that behind what appear to be passive or mischievous grins are intellectual and artistic surprises of some moment. The servant leader finds it easy to say "sir" not just to men of station and privilege but to the farmer just out of the field and the city worker who collects his garbage each Tuesday.

A Hospitality to Hostility. In another chapter, I have suggested that one of the roles of the academic administrator is to absorb the hostility of the ill-informed and ill-mannered. Even the most altruistic leader will find the challenge of mistrust and suspicion a formidable one.

For example, a friend, dean of a large college of liberal arts, is active in community and civic affairs. He regularly takes part in Little Theatre productions, contributes articles to the morning newspaper, and is active on several civic boards. His civic involvements and visibility bring a number of benefits to his college.

An angry faculty member who had disagreed with one of the dean's recent decisions accused the dean of being involved in civic affairs only to fatten his résumé for a more lucrative and prestigious administrative post. The servant leader is not beyond being hurt by such accusations but learns patience, perhaps recalling these lines by Marcus Aurelius:

> if a man should stand by a limpid pure spring and curse it, the spring does not stop sending up pure water; and if he should cast dirt and filth into it, it will speedily disperse them and wash them out, and will not be at all polluted. How then shall you possess a perpetual fountain? By imbuing yourself hourly with freedom, benevolence, simplicity and modesty.

An Expectation of Opportunity in Interruptions. In one of the more informative empirical studies of management, Henry Mintzberg suggests in *The Nature of Managerial Work* (1973) that activities of most managers are "characterized by brevity, variety, and fragmentation" (p. 51). Leaders are men and women always on the way to somewhere − to the office, to the faculty council meeting, to the governor's office, to a meeting of the board. And if they can find a moment, perhaps they are on the way to the executive water closet. Leaders are inevitably late to meetings, which is accepted as an indication of how busy they are. And when the trajectory of the executive is interrupted, tension can be high and empathy low.

However, the servant leader looks for opportunity in the interruption. Just a moment's hesitation and more care in listening would have let me learn of Thelma's accident. A little less hectic pace would have enabled me to give Steve's idea a more courteous ear. A little slower walk through Bronson Hall might have alerted me to Dave's pending retirement. Listening longer, I could have appreciated more fully the anger of the student before me.

I have a new resolution − to walk more slowly from my car in the morning to the office. I have in mind not the direct and speedy trip that I usually take but a wandering one like the little boy takes on the way to school, stopping to gaze at a morning butterfly or a spider building its web − except I am looking for moments of hurt or joy in the lives of the men and women for whom I am responsible.

A Devotion to Principle Beyond Self. A few years ago I described a mentor in my life as follows:

> A college dean spent fifteen years in the same position. He was not upwardly mobile. He did not become vice president nor president. He was modestly active in church and community. He arrived at work most mornings at 8:00 or 8:30 and left most afternoons by 5:00. On special occasions, such as registration, he could be found at work after

hours. And on Saturday mornings he took coffee with students and friends.

During the time he was at work, the careful discipline of his time, a trusting investment in a good staff, the force of his commitment, and the authority of his personality inspired qualitative program improvements throughout his college. He was near to the concerns of students, patient with the troubled, and summary in his treatment of the arrogant. The quality of his judgment and caring was clear to all. He was confidant to clerk typists, students, faculty, administrator colleagues, and the president of the institution.

The strength of his conviction was tested by more than one opponent, and his honesty refreshingly different. He could make artistic and effective application of tension and conflict because they occurred in relationships that were nurtured and prepared by stability and security. A quiet professional whose leadership was not to be measured in terms of growth, not in his own mobility, not in the record of his involvements, and not in a rush of activity, but in the ideals he engendered in the lives of students and colleagues. When he retired from the university, the accounts receivable carried no record of his contribution; but the affection carried in the hearts of those who knew him revealed that he possessed the complete wisdom of true managerial artist. (Bogue and Saunders 1976)

Here was a man devoted to principles of service, to principles that went beyond his private welfare and ambition. Perhaps he had read yet other lines from history:

> In a little while all but the mightiest of the Great Kings were forgotten, and all their royal palaces were in ruins under the drifting sands. Two hundred years after its capture, Xenophon's Ten Thousand marched over the mounds that had been Nineveh, and never suspected that these were the site of the ancient metropolis that had ruled half the world. Not a stone remained visible of all the temples with which Assyria's pious warriors had sought to beautify their greatest capital. Even Ashur, the everlasting God, was dead. (Durant, p. 284)

A Sensitive Use of Authority. Earlier I spoke of the use of power. The sensitive and artistic application of authority is a mark of the servant leader. This concept is beautifully stated in Robert Greenleaf's *Servant Leadership* (1977):

> A new moral principle is emerging which holds that the only authority deserving one's allegiance is that which is freely and knowingly granted by the led to the leader in response to, and in proportion to, the clearly evident servant stature of the leader. Those who choose to follow this principle will not casually accept the authority of existing institutions. Rather, they will freely respond only to individuals who are chosen as leaders because they are proven and trusted as servants. To

the extent that this principle prevails in the future, the only truly viable institutions will be those that are predominantly servant-led. (p. 100)

The Nurture of the Service Motive

Recently I made a trip to Olympia, Washington, to give a commencement address to Evergreen State College. As usual, I waited until the last moment to complete planning for the trip. A quick visit to the nearby automatic bank teller furnished a little cash for the trip. At the bank I was not greeted by a friendly teller at 2:00 p.m. on a Sunday afternoon; but I did not seem to miss that personal attention as the money machine accepted my card, recognized it among several thousand in Shreveport, printed out "Good afternoon, Mr. Bogue" on the screen, checked the balance in my account (always an anxious moment), delivered the cash I needed, and then presented a menu of other services to see if I might need any of these.

At 4:30 p.m. that same afternoon I boarded Delta Flight 883 to Seattle. Following a friendly reception at the baggage counter and by the stewardess at the door of the Boeing 767, I settled into my seat for the three-hour flight. On the bulkhead in front of me I noticed a silver plaque inscribed "The Spirit of Delta." The plaque described how this particular aircraft had been donated to Delta Airlines by current and former employees. I reflected on the spirit of devotion and ownership that had motivated such an act by a company's employees.

As I work on this chapter, I think back on a few days of renewal during a family vacation. One of the more pleasant moments was a quiet evening at Hudson's Landing Restaurant on Hilton Head Island. One of the three persons waiting on our table was a cheerful young man who had only the simplest of tasks to perform — keeping the water glasses and coffee cups filled. This is not an assignment that industrial psychologists have been able to enrich very much. However, this young man had invested a menial assignment with his personal cheer. As he moved among the tables, one could sense an elevating effect radiating from his warm smile and cheerful comments. This young man will bring customers back to that restaurant. He had the service motive.

How do we encourage this service motive among our colleagues? The first step is to inventory our own attitudes, to model the service motive in our own lives. But there are additional leadership steps possible. Let us attend to a few of these.

Find Out What Folks Think of Services. In Chapter Five, I treated the theme of quality assurance. Here is an opportunity to affirm that leadership obligation. What do we know about what people think of institutional services — in the classroom, in the registrar's office, in the library, and in the bookstore? What profile would we uncover if we inventoried the sources of service complaints in our colleges and universities on such matters as rude treatment by administrative staff, offices closed during times of student need, disputes over refunds, faculty unavailable during office hours, or complicated forms and procedures?

Many industries are making use of "disguised observers" to find out what makes their organizations go. In Chapter Two, I cited the story of sane patients being admitted to mental hospitals to ascertain what level of treatment was accorded patients and how discriminating were the professional staff in their judgments of patients' mental health. What would we find if we asked a small group of students to keep notes on their experiences for a term and then give us a report on what the university looked like from a client perspective? What does registration look like to the new student just walking in the door? Is purchasing your first set of texts an intimidating experience? What is the impression after the first week of classes? After the term ends? In his provocative little book, *Up the Organization* (1970), former Avis Corporation President Robert Townsend suggests:

> When you're off on a business trip or a vacation, pretend you're a customer. Telephone some part of your organization and ask for help. You'll run into some real horror shows. Don't blow up and ask for name, rank, and serial number — you're trying to correct, not punish. If it happens on a call to the Dubuque office, just suggest to the manager (through channels, dummy) that he make a few test calls himself. Then try calling yourself up and see what indignities you've built into your own defenses. (p. 31)

One caveat. We need to remember who keeps score and how. To illustrate, if accountants are keeping score on bank tellers on how they balance out at the end of the day, one can hardly fault this indicator of effectiveness. However, if the tellers are technically flawless, balance out correctly every day, but are rude or apathetic with customers, you could finish with a bank with debits and credits in good balance but with no customers to serve. Here is that counsel from another perspective.

> It would be useful if the definition of "productivity" — especially in service industries — was broadened to include at least courtesy and style of performance — particularly because the long-term effectiveness of the organization depends on service. Because the performance of employees in service organizations is directed at animate objects rather than the nonfeeling, nonresponsive raw material handled in the manufacturing world, the appropriate judge of performance should be those who are served. (Schneider 1980, p. 53)

The leadership obligations seem simple enough. Ask your students and your community for their opinion.

Equip Staff with Knowledge. While a sour attitude can prevent us from rendering courteous service in our classrooms and offices, so can a lack of knowledge. "I don't know" can be quite as damaging as "I don't care."

Business and auxiliary staff who have not been trained for their work can find it easy to mask their lack of knowledge with officious or sarcastic responses to questions from students and faculty. But the dangers of inadequate knowledge can be found in other places as well. Let's move to the academic arena.

In a recent workshop on academic advising, I watched Fred Alexander of the American College Testing program guide faculty in the improvement of advising skills. He distributed to the faculty the achievement, activity, and career interests profiles of four "hypothetical entering students." After going over the students' backgrounds, he invited faculty to comment on what program advice they might give those entering students. After a lively discussion, Fred brought in the four "hypothetical" students, who were actually enrolled in the institution as juniors, and asked them to tell what advice they had been given during the five or six semesters they had been enrolled. The revelations for the day were humorous, disturbing, and informing.

Search for Ways to Automate Services. How about a friendly automatic clerk, similar to automatic bank tellers, in the admissions office or registrar's office and available to students 24 hours a day? Students and potential students interacting with this service could be provided a menu of services such as how to be admitted, including the option of completing an admissions application online; how to drop and add a course; what financial aid is available; whom to contact for information on residency classification; and how to leave a number for service call back on any question not adequately answered.

Automation in the service sector has been nicely described in *Long Range Planning* by David Collier (1983). Every service industry in the country – airlines, insurance companies, banks, hospitals – is racing to automate more of their direct contact customer services. We have yet to put our imagination fully to work on the same question in schools and colleges.

What would the installation of an automatic irrigation system save? Will the installation of an energy management system reduce our energy costs? Should we combine secretarial services into a word-processing center? How long will it be before students can access the library from their home computer? There are encouraging ventures already under way on these and other service productivity improvements.

Promote Ownership in the Life of the Institution. Why did Delta employees give their company an airplane? Presumably because they felt that their own welfare was linked with that of the company, and because they had a sense of pride and ownership in the company. We do not have to believe that every single employee salutes the company every day to appreciate what a unifying spirit does to an institution. Can such a spirit be nurtured in the university? Yes! But the leadership challenges are complex and formidable.

Here is a brilliant and devoted full professor of English who has given 20 years of his life to the university. He is known for his competent and caring investment in his students. He is known for a range of civic and professional involvements. Even with a full load of teaching, he has managed to publish two books. He loves the university and his community. In the current market he is not very mobile. And because of family roots, he does not want to be mobile. But it hurts even his large heart when a newly minted computer science Ph.D. is offered a contract at a salary $15,000 above his own, when one of his recent graduates goes to work as an accountant for the city at a salary only $2,000 less than his, when the state cannot manage a salary raise this year, when the state higher education commission turns down a newly proposed master's degree program that he had a role in developing, when 20 automobiles and buses are available to transport athletic teams but he cannot travel to a regional meeting to present a paper.

Orchestrating the use of authority and rewards in a modern school or college is a challenge for the servant leader. Respect, trust, involvement – these provide the foundation for continued ownership among the men and women whose minds and hearts furnish meaning to the word "university."

A Quest for Leadership Fulfillment – A Summary

The quest for self-fulfillment is a common journey for those who lead and those who follow. But there is a difference. The leader's style, model, and values determine the extent to which those who follow are able to achieve self-fulfillment.

It may come to us in a flash of revelation. It may sneak up on us gradually. It may make a bloody and difficult entrance. It may come in a gentle dawning. Eventually, the mature leader will discover that power, prestige, and possessions do not yield lasting fulfillment. Power and pay cannot nourish the soul of the artist administrator. Only a devotion to service can do that.

Arrogance is an enemy of leadership.

References

Bogue, E.G., and Saunders, Robert L. *The Educational Manager: Artist and Practitioner*. Worthington, Ohio: Charles A Jones, 1976.

Boyer, Ernest L., and Hechinger, Fred M. *Higher Learning in the Nation's Service*. Washington, D.C.: Carnegie Foundation for the Advancement of Teaching, 1981.

Cartwright, Dorwin. "Influence, Leadership, and Control." In *Handbook of Organizations*, edited by J.G. March. Chicago: Rand McNally, 1965.

Collier, David A. "The Service Sector Revolution: The Automation of Services." *Long Range Planning* 16 (1983):10-20.

Demerath, Nicholas J., et al. *Power, Presidents, and Professors*. New York: Basic Books, 1967.

Durant, Will. *Our Oriental Heritage, The Story of Civilization*. Vol. 1. New York: Simon & Schuster, 1954.

Fisher, James L. *Power of the Presidency*. New York: American Council on Education, Macmillan, 1984.

Frankl, Victor. *Man's Search for Meaning: An Introduction to Logotherapy*. Boston: Beacon Press, 1959.

French, J.R.P., Jr., and Raven, B. "The Bases of Social Power." In *Studies in Social Power*, edited by D. Cartwright. Ann Arbor: University of Michigan, Institute for Social Research, 1959.

Greenleaf, Robert K. *Servant Leadership*. New York: Paulist Press, 1977.

Hamilton, J. Wallace. *The Thunder of Bare Feet*. Westwood, N.J.: Fleming H. Revell, 1964.

Highet, Gilbert. *The Immortal Profession*. New York: Weybright and Talley, 1976.

Keller, George. *Academic Strategy: The Management Revolution in American Higher Education*. Baltimore: Johns Hopkins University Press, 1983.

Mintzberg, Henry. *The Nature of Managerial Work*. New York: Harper & Row, 1973.

Russell, Bertrand. *Authority and the Individual*. New York: Simon & Schuster, 1949.

Schneider, Benjamin. "The Service Organizations: Climate is Crucial." *Organizational Dynamics* (Autumn 1980):53.

Szanton, Peter. *Not Well Advised*. New York: Russell Sage, 1981.

Townsend, Robert. *Up the Organization*. New York: Alfred A. Knopf, 1970.

Chapter Eight

The Productivity Imperative

Treat people as adults. Treat them as partners; treat them with dignity; treat them with respect. Treat them — *not capital spending and automation* — *as the primary sources of productivity gains.*

— Thomas J. Peters and Robert H. Waterman, Jr.
In Search of Excellence.

The demand for efficiency and accountability is legitimate. Higher Education has a clear responsibility to operate efficiently and to report its costs and results to the American People in ways that transcend the tired rhetoric of commencement speeches and slick brochures....But the call for accountability cannot be satisfied if all the results of higher education must be reduced to neat quantitative terms, preferably with dollar signs attached.

— Howard Bowen
Professor of Economics and Education
Claremont Graduate School

Productivity is an issue of national concern. One would have to be a hermit not to see the attention being accorded this management concern in our nation. Comparisons of industrial production show that the United States has lagged behind a number of countries in recent years. For example, the *Bulletin of International Economic Conditions* (1984) shows that the average annual growth rate in industrial production for Japan in the period 1973-83 was 2.2%, whereas for the United States during that same period the growth rate was 1.3%.

How does this translate for American business? Writing in *Industrial Renaissance* (1983), Abernathy and others indicate that the cost advantage in the Japanese automobile industry is more than the difference in labor cost between Japan and the United States. The labor cost differential accounts for less than half the cost advantage; the remaining advantage derives from labor and capital productivity. "A small Japanese car, packed into a

108

freighter and shipped across the Pacific, lands on the American dock with a cost advantage over comparable U.S. products of something between $1,200 and $1,500, conservatively estimated" (p. 63). These data are now a few years old, and there is reason to believe that the U.S. automobile industry is back in the race. The farmer who looks out his back door in middle Tennessee and sees a massive new Nissan truck and car manufacturing plant at work and a resident of Marysville, Ohio, watching a new Honda factory go to work know that productivity and competition are international matters.

Editorials in the *Wall Street Journal*, books on productivity in both profit sector (LeBoeuf 1982) and service sector (Heaton 1977), the emergence of productivity centers for business and universities, and the publication of journals such as *National Productivity Review* are more than adequate signals of our national interest in this theme. In *The Productivity Challenge* (1982), Michael LeBoeuf provides a tongue-in-cheek explanation for our decline in productivity:

> The population of the United States is 225 million but there are 63 million retired, leaving 162 million to do the work. Those too young to work total 86 million, leaving 76 million to do the work. Then there are 36 million employed by the federal government and that leaves 40 million to do the work. The number in the armed forces is 13 million, which leaves 27 million to do the work. Deduct 25,765,000, the number employed by state and local government and the 520,000 in hospitals and the like and you have 715,000 left to do the work. But of these, 462,000 are bums and vagrants who won't work. So that leaves 253,000. Now it may interest you to know that there are 252,998 in jail, so that leaves two people to carry the load. That's you and I, and I'm taking a week's vacation effective tomorrow. So carry on. You will be absolutely terrific! (pp. 10-11)

As I begin the day in my office, I ply through several memos on my desk. One of these is from women faculty concerned with the condition of restroom facilities in one of our buildings. Attached to the memo is a sample of graffiti from the women's restroom (in which I discover that the Chancellor's name has been disparaged). The call to productivity sounds from a distant trumpet as I ponder the range of issues, great and small, that requires the attention of an administrator.

Turning to the morning issue of the *Shreveport Times* for 18 September 1984, I find that the productivity issue has moved a little closer to home. Here in Shreveport, according to a front-page story, both labor and management are joined in a common concern related to productivity in the local AT&T Consumer Products plant, which employs more than 6,000 and is one of the larger manufacturers of telephones in the nation and in the world. However, anyone who recently has walked into Sears, Radio Shack, or a local department store knows that AT&T is no longer the sole manufacturer of telephones.

This morning's story concerns a letter issued to union members at the plant by the head of the local International Brotherhood of Electrical Workers. The essence of the letter is that, at the moment, it is costing this plant $1.08 to produce $1.00 in sales. The arithmetic is plain to all, and the letter enlists the aid of plant workers in the improvement of productivity at the plant.

A newly designed and more automated assembly line has begun operating at the plant but is not fully at capacity. It offers promise of increased productivity for the plant and is a potent instrument for meeting the challenge of international competition. Meanwhile, labor and management engage in a common challenge. If plant productivity cannot be improved by better technology, better management, and the dedication and skill of the workers, then thousands of jobs may disappear in the face of this competition. (In the few short months between the time I wrote this original and the time I am correcting proofs, the local situation has changed dramatically. The AT&T plant has moved one of its assembly lines to Singapore and has laid off several hundred employees in Shreveport.)

Some five miles away, those of us at the university greet the smiling but sleepy faces of our students this morning, having thought little about productivity and more about salary levels and bathroom graffiti. A few faculty, such as Professor LeBoeuf at the University of New Orleans, are writing books and articles about productivity. The extent to which their talent is turned inward to examine the same issue in education institutions is unknown.

However, a quick search shows that the issue of productivity and efficiency in schools and universities is not a new theme, at least for purposes of discussion if not for action. I walk over to my professional bookshelf and pull down five major publications now a decade old: *The More Effective Use of Resources* (1972), *Efficiency in Universities: The La Paz Papers* (1974), *Institutional Efficiency in State Systems of Public Higher Education* (1975), *Increasing Productivity in Higher Education* (1974), and *Productivity: Burden of Success* (1973). The last monograph carries an interesting observation:

> The word productivity itself is unwelcome in many academic conversations as wholly inappropriate to higher learning. But compared to many of the other service activities, education has a clear production function in generating new knowledge and in creating a pool of more able individuals. It is not just a facilitative, restorative, or preventive enterprise, even though its product of value-added properties may be hard to capture (Toombs, p. 3).

While academics debate whether productivity is a business issue whose questions are unwelcome and unworthy in a university setting, we continue to steal resources from ourselves and our publics through inept management and narrow vision. As with quality assurance, we too often prefer to debate than to act.

Here is a devoted employee in the Office of Institutional Research for a large state university. The office wall is covered with impressive sheets of white poster board that tell you at a moment's notice what classes are occupying what rooms at what times. This is the university's facilities scheduling center. With this clerk's salary and supporting expenses, it costs the university about $25,000 per year to operate this center. That the same data profile could be produced with an hour's formatting and programming, and with little computer operating time, has escaped the attention of both faculty and administrators. When the vice president for administration finally discovers this "productivity" issue, he has to fight the state civil service machinery to abolish the classified position.

Next door to the Office of Institutional Research is the registrar's office. Here more than a hundred clerks, assorted supervisors, and a hundred unanswered phone calls extract more than a million dollars each year from the university's operating budget − for a cluster of student services that are delivered for a third of that sum at another university similar in size, history, mission, and community setting. The faculty have yet to discover that fresh management could return perhaps a third to a half of this million dollars to the university. And the administrative amateur who sits on the top of this mess has neither the ability nor the courage to engage the productivity issue.

What exactly are the leadership impediments to understanding and action on the productivity issue in colleges and universities? What are the signals that more vigorous leadership attention is needed? And are there any incentives for a more aggressive approach to productivity?

A Productivity Definition

Before we try to answer these questions, perhaps we should ensure a common understanding on just what we mean by productivity. In simplest form, productivity is the relationship of outputs to inputs. A technical definition given by Sink and others (1984) is "the ratio of quantities of output [goods and services] from an organizational system over a period of time to quantities of input resources consumed by that organizational system for that period of time; or, the ratio of quantity at the desired level to resources actually consumed" (p. 265). In their definition, productivity is a concept that integrates concern for effectiveness, efficiency, and quality.

Effectiveness is an output issue. Did we accomplish what our goals, objectives, and programs indicated we hoped to accomplish? Efficiency is

111

primarily an input issue, defined as the "ratio of resources expected to be consumed . . . to resources actually consumed." And quality asks questions of whether that product is fit for use. Quality, therefore, is a concept linking both input and output.

My own thinking may be dissatisfying to the true scholar, as I tend to blur the terms productivity and efficiency. What I have in mind for education leadership, however, is doing a better quality job of educating our students with the same or reduced resources.

A simple example of elements involved in productivity is as follows. Suppose that Grandfather Ted has taken to the manufacture of toy wooden trucks in his retirement years. He makes regular visits to shopping malls where he sells these trucks. He finds that the demand is more than he can satisfy from his simple woodworking shop in his garage at home. How do we increase his productivity? We can send Grandfather Ted to school where he will learn to operate woodworking machines that will improve his output of toy trucks, provided he also purchases these machines after he has learned to operate them. We can redesign his shop and perhaps hire two or three students to assist after school, assigning each of them some small portion of the production and assembly task that they can master in short order. We may also install a personal computer to help in charting the manufacturing steps and in controlling inventory, accounting, and billing.

One caveat. We may find that Grandfather Ted would rather not do any of this, since that was what he was doing before he retired from IBM. He just wants to build a few trucks whenever he feels like it, enjoy the simple pleasure of carving them with his own hands, and take a moment's pleasure in the smile of a young boy who has become the proud owner of a hand-crafted product.

Now let's proceed with a more detailed analysis of the productivity puzzle.

The Productivity Puzzle

Michael LeBoeuf, a professor of management at the University of New Orleans, has identified some of the pieces of the productivity puzzle. His ideas are worth examining by those holding administrative posts in education. Following is a synopsis of the 12 pieces of the puzzle from LeBoeuf's *The Productivity Challenge* (1983) and a few comments on each:

1. *A Lack of National Commitment.* Once the acknowledged economic leader of the world, our national complacency has been shaken in recent years by the rapidly increasing productivity of other nations compared to our own sluggish growth. What can we say about leadership in education on the same issue? Will the current and projected record of federal and state finance force more attention on productivity in the educational sector?

2. *A Lack of Incentives for Productivity.* In this nation, labor-saving technology and processes have often been seen as a threat to jobs, leaving

management and labor locked in conflict over job security. The important difference now is that international competition may mean no jobs if management and labor cannot join in common concern. Those of us in public education have not had much competition. Will that condition remain? Will educational ventures of corporations remain centered on their own educational needs or will we see movements of investor-owned companies into the educational marketplace similar to what has happened in hospitals?

3. *Aging Plant and Equipment.* How this problem has affected the U.S. steel and automobile industries is well known. These and other industries are in a race to modernize plants, managing the painful steps required to change plants or to close down plants. Will education institutions with aging physical plants accept the challenge of dealing with growing maintenance and energy costs?

4. *Foreign Competition.* The impact of foreign competition is apparent to anyone who looks at the sales figures of foreign products such as automobiles and consumer electronics. Here is one area where American higher education may have a market advantage. According to the U.S. Department of Education, there were 330,000 nonresident alien students enrolled in American higher education in 1982. Higher education may be one "product" where we can maintain a favorable competitive posture.

5. *Skyrocketing Energy Prices.* The winners in energy are those who charge higher prices and the losers are those who pay. America has been losing and the Arabians winning recently, though there are some encouraging trends in our national energy consumption and production capacity. The college or university that has shifted its power plant from coal to oil and back to coal again knows this cost challenge. The university anticipating a 25% increase in its utility budget in a year when its budget remains relatively flat knows the productivity challenge that comes in reconciling the question of whether higher paid faculty will work in colder buildings.

6. *A Research and Development Slump.* Today Japan and the Soviet Union are producing engineers and other technical manpower at rates higher than the U.S. A failure to make investments in research and development today is a mistake that cannot be reversed in a year or two. Here again is where higher education has an important, though not a monopolistic, role in the improvement of our national productivity.

7. *Changing Nature of the Workforce.* We have yet to assess fully the social impact of the influx of female labor into the U.S. workforce. Some say that the increase in working mothers is having a deleterious effect on the young, as "latchkey" children return to empty homes. Also, a relatively low-paid female workforce is no longer available to our schools and colleges as women find access to and upward mobility in other professions and work fields.

8. *The Decline of Standards in Public Education.* In LeBoeuf's vision, schools and colleges in this nation are part of the productivity problem.

We are being hindered by low standards, inadequately prepared teachers, and too much bureaucracy. Most educators know that the problems of U.S. society are not so simplistic as to be traced to schools and colleges alone − independent of changing social, family, and economic conditions. Nevertheless, it is not easy to accept that we may indeed be a part of the problem. We can be a part of the solution.

9. *Burdensome Bureaucracies*. Here is one part of the puzzle to which educators can relate as much as their business and industrial colleagues. Some professions will not appreciate LeBoeuf's observation that Japan has one attorney for every 10,000 people, whereas the U.S. has 20 for every 10,000 people. College presidents who spend hours answering attorneys' letters on both serious and frivolous matters will enjoy that comparison, however.

10. *Inept Management*. Short-run mentality, lack of vision, depersonalization, indecision − these are some of the criticisms LeBoeuf makes about American management. No one can afford to live in a glass house on this issue. We have our own work cut out for us in education management.

11. *Labor-Management Conflict*. Anyone who reads the history of labor and management relations in this nation should find current times of interest. The recent experiences of Braniff Airlines and Chrysler Motor Company make fascinating case studies, as does the AT&T illustration cited in this chapter, on the changing character of labor-management relations. The lessons from industry should not go unheeded by those of us in education.

12. *Counter-Productive Values*. LeBoeuf paints America as the "now" generation, reinforcing a point made in Naisbitt's *Megatrends*. The tendency to sacrifice long-term goals to make the short run look good, when combined with our growing reluctance to take risks, bodes ill for our economic future. The picture that emerges is one of a nearsighted, security-conscious, depersonalized nation that does not want to take chances. Do these descriptors fit education leadership as well?

Let me enlarge on LeBoeuf's final point concerning our values and productivity. I have in front of me the 20 September 1984 issue of the *Wall Street Journal* and the 3 October 1984 issue of the *Chronicle of Higher Education*. The *Journal* carries a front-page story with the headline, "How Frigitemp Sank After It Was Looted by Top Management." I read that Mervyn Silver, the president of Frigitemp, Gerald Lee, the company chairman, and apparently other company officials admit to having made millions of dollars in payoffs to get business. They say that they took kickbacks from suppliers, embezzled company funds, exaggerated earnings in reports to shareholders, and provided prostitutes to customers. Such violations of business integrity affect our national productivity.

The *Chronicle* story is about the former president of Western Wyoming College and two other administrators who have been charged with four felony counts of unauthorized use of moneys. On page 2 of this same issue of the *Chronicle* is this headline: "Colorado Auditor Accuses 6 Colleges on Overcharges." Those who read the *Chronicle* on a regular basis know that these are not the first stories to appear concerning unethical administration in colleges and universities. The prostitution of leadership integrity is, in my judgment, far more damaging than sapping productivity. And I will have more to say about why in Chapter 10.

Productivity Impediments in Education

Why is it that conversations on productivity are so unwelcome among educators? Some of the suspicion and cynicism is no doubt the result of differing value perspectives among different academic disciplines in a university. Our faculty council at Louisiana State University in Shreveport recently debated the merit of "self nomination" for eligibility to participate in a program of outstanding faculty awards. A professor of history addressed the impropriety of faculty nominating themselves for such an award. A professor of business seemed more concerned about the tax liability if one won the award. Such differences in perspective, even on minor issues, are often later embellished in coffee lounge conversation to illustrate how crassly utilitarian business faculty are and how naive liberal arts faculty are.

A 20-year full professor of philosophy making only $27,000, while a new associate professor of accounting makes $37,000, is unlikely to be charitable about proposals for improving academic productivity — even though such proposals might eventually contribute to increases in his own salary.

Some faculty members, fond of exclaiming about the dire consequences of entrusting the future of the university to "business number crunchers," use the illustration below that purports to show what would happen if the management of a symphony orchestra were given over to an efficiency expert:

> For considerable periods the three oboe players had nothing to do. By spreading their work over the whole of the concert, peaks of activity could be reduced, and the number reduced to one.
>
> The entire violin section of twenty frequently were playing identical notes, clearly an unnecessary duplication. The staff of this section should be reduced. If a larger volume of sound is required, electronic amplifiers may be employed.
>
> Considerable effort was absorbed in the execution of thirty-second notes in some of the more technical passages. A frivolous refinement, these may be rounded to sixteenth notes. Of course, this would render the passages more simple and permit the use of trainees and lower grade operatives — a move of obvious efficiency.
>
> Further, there was extensive repetition of some musical passages. No useful purpose is served by repeating on the woodwinds a theme

already well handled by the strings. A careful pruning of the redundant passages could reduce the concert time of two hours and thirty minutes to forty-five minutes. And then, of course, there would also be no need for an intermission, thus reducing the rental time for the concert hall (Umbeck 1970).

The first objection to the consideration of productivity issues is educators' suspicion of both the values and the instruments of profit-sector enterprise. Another objection is that the outputs of education are not as easily defined as the outputs of industrial enterprise. The production of trucks, transformers, and telephones, all manufactured within a 10-mile radius of our campus in Shreveport, is more easily measured than the "production" of educated men and women at our university.

Still another difficulty is the view that educational quality always has to be linked with higher costs. For example, it costs well over ten times as much to attend some private universities in this nation as it does for a student to attend Louisiana State University in Shreveport. For some, the cost description of an institution is also a quality description. Obviously this is not a linkage that I accept, but for some in higher education the cost/quality linkage is an uncontestable relationship.

Productivity indices may tell us something about the "more or less" of an enterprise, but do they tell us about the "good and the bad"? If my secretary can produce 40 memos with our new information-processing system in the same time she used to produce 20 memos, then I might argue that our productivity is vastly improved. That productivity index, however, does not say anything about whether I should have written all those memos rather than using the phone, or whether this shower of paper is helpful for the functioning of the university. It is entirely possible that the negative impact of a single carelessly worded memo could create more organizational ferment and financial mischief than the cost of 10 new information-processing systems.

A final concern is the often-stated view that our schools could be more effective and more productive if they were run in a more businesslike way. According to this view, the rough-and-tumble world of competition in the profit sector is driven by the incentive of efficiency, whereas secure public-sector executives do not have this incentive.

I remember a major investor-owned hospital corporate executive proudly announcing that executives in his company were now using compact cars for their business travel rather than luxury sedans. This statement was made at a corporate retreat held in the Grand Cayman Islands in the Caribbean. It may be true that a patient's bill is lower because the vice president now uses a Cavalier instead of a Cadillac. On the other hand, that advantage may be lost on the patient when he hears about the retreat being held in the Grand Caymans instead of Kansas City or Indianapolis.

116

Despite the impediments discussed above, higher education is beginning to grapple with the productivity issue. I am looking now at two recent articles; one, titled "Increasing Productivity in the Community College: A National Effort," describes a national productivity center in the Dallas Community College District, which deals with such issues as energy conservation, student attrition, and staff utilization (O'Banion 1984). The second, titled "Carnegie-Mellon Chief Foresees Three-Year Bachelor's Programs," describes President Richard Cyert's effort to bring every Carnegie-Mellon student into contact with computers and gives his assessment of the instructional impact of that effort (Cyert 1984). There may be good reasons why educators have been reluctant to come to terms with productivity issues, but some promising initiatives are being made. What are the incentives for those initiatives? Let's turn our attention there.

Productivity Imperatives and Incentives

Some of the gross indicators of higher education productivity in the last decade or so can be found in the 1984 edition of *The Condition of Education*, a publication of the National Center for Education Statistics. A review of these indicators on enrollment, staffing, financing, and degrees conferred reveals the following:

1. In the decade of the Seventies, there was a dramatic increase in higher education enrollment, a 45% increase in the years 1970-1982.
2. During that same period, there was a staffing increase, at least for teaching ranks, of 52%. However, the majority of that increase was in part-time faculty, an increase of 140%. Full-time staff increased only 28%.
3. The federal government contributed a little less and the states more to the cost of education. It is important to note, however, that these data do not include student-aid accounts. For example, federal government appropriations for postsecondary student aid rose from $0.5 billion in 1970-71 to $6.3 billion in 1981-82.
4. Expenditures per FTE student remained relatively constant, as measured in buying power and constant dollars.
5. The pattern of degrees awarded between 1970-82 varied: a 13% increase in bachelor degrees, a 28% increase in masters degrees, a 2% increase in doctoral degrees, and a whopping 90% increase in first professional degrees such as law and medicine.

American higher education has accommodated these enrollment increases, generated these increases in degrees granted — especially in graduate and first professional degrees — with essentially a level expenditure per FTE student. This is, I believe, a pleasant tribute to college productivity. The additional funding now being appropriated for education by several states is further testimony to the wisdom of our nation in looking to the future.

And what of that future? The 1984 edition of *The Condition of Education* furnishes projections through 1992 for several areas in higher education, but there is no projection for anticipated revenue. I am not convinced that we will continue to see the dramatic increases in federal or state revenues that we experienced during the Seventies. The public concern over the current federal deficit of more than $200 billion, the difficulty that many states have encountered in meeting basic services, and the future demand occasioned by current large investments in personnel and salaries lead me to the conclusion that college leadership would be wise to look for ways in which to get more mileage for the dollar.

Higher education leadership already has been responding to the productivity call. One prominent example is the program of the National Association of College and University Business Officers (NACUBO) of Cost Reduction Incentive Awards. In 1984, the ninth year of that award program, 47 institutions received monetary awards ranging from $7,500 to $10,000. This program is co-sponsored by the United States Steel Foundation (NACUBO/USSF 1984).

A partial list of the winners for 1984 show where savings are being realized:

Ultrasound Device to Detect Faulty Steam Traps — estimated to save $285,000 per year at Indiana University-Purdue University at Indianapolis.

Using Credit Cards for Small Purchase Orders — estimated to save $118,000 at Lane Community College.

A Travel Management Program — estimated to save $300,000 per year at Columbia University.

Silver Reflectors on Fluorescent Light Fixtures — estimated to save $300,000 per year at the University of California at Berkeley.

Consolidation of Student and Business Services — estimated to save $92,000 at Friends University.

These illustrations of increased productivity and efficiency clearly reveal that colleges and universities can achieve cost savings, especially in administrative and support areas. What is not so clear is whether colleges and universities can and will achieve cost savings in the one program area where they spend the most money — in instruction.

We are on the threshold of what many believe to be the most dramatic change since the Industrial Revolution — the Information Revolution. We are not far from the time when students can just purchase a chip from the campus bookstore and take the library home. Or they can use their home computer and modem to link up with a main frame storage unit on the campus. Or they may not come to campus at all!

In a speech carried in the 1 May 1984 issue of *Vital Speeches of the Day*, David F. Linowes indicated that:

> There are more than 300,000 classroom computers now available in public schools and by 1985 that number will double.

> The PLATO education system developed at the University of Illinois is being modified to increase its capacity a hundredfold, so that the number of terminals that can be accessed by the new system will rise from 1,200 to 150,000.

> Atari has introduced what it heralds as the "world's first electronic university," offering 170 courses in such fields as art, finance, and business management.

The possibilities of using computers to facilitate and enhance teaching and learning in every field from poetry to physics are staggering. A recent set of working papers produced by the American Association for Higher Education details current trends on several campuses and points to the changes possible for a future that is already here (Tucker 1983-84). Carnegie-Mellon President Richard Cyert says, "With software programs designed to give students more sophisticated information more quickly than traditional approaches, all the necessary work toward a bachelor's degree could be completed in three years − or students could stay for four years and receive a masters degree."

Those who remember the heralded promises of instructional television of yesteryear will adopt a wait-and-see attitude on this prediction for computers. Will the computer in the classroom and the office actually promote productivity improvements, or will they cost us more money? The potential of the computer for building on solid instructional and motivation theories, for delivering facts, concepts, and relationships, for reducing personnel costs in favor of capital costs, is, I think, a potential of some moment − one that will allow our schools to improve both instructional effectiveness and efficiency. As with any tool, the question may reside less with the quality and nature of the tool than with the intelligence, values, and courage of those who put the tool to work.

There are other incentives for the improvement of productivity in our schools. The first of these is a simple matter of public duty. Every public manager is obligated, at least in my value system, to manage his or her enterprise in the most effective manner possible with the resources available. Whether a city manager or a college president, there is a responsibility not to waste public funds, to ensure that public dollars purchase the most bang for the buck. The college president who misuses public moneys, the registrar who operates an office that is a management nightmare, the dean who is careless and sloppy in his attention to class sizes − these leaders are not meeting that obligation.

A second incentive is entirely selfish in origin. Resources made available from increased efficiency and productivity in support programs and other administrative activities can be redirected to instructional programs. An example of this is illustrated in the table below, which shows the typical percentages of our expenditures allocated by function at Louisiana State University in Shreveport compared to the Southern Association of Colleges and Schools (SACS) percentages.

Function	LSU-S Percentage	SACS Percentage
Instruction	54.1	43.7
Research	0.2	1.9
Public Service	1.9	2.5
Academic Support	13.0	9.1
Student Services	5.2	6.8
Institutional Support	14.3	15.5
Operation and Maintenance of Plant	9.9	14.1
Scholarships	1.4	6.4

The management history of the university allows it to place a relatively higher percentage of its operation budget in instruction and such academic support services as the library. Where do we get these extra funds? The table shows that we are spending less than other Southern colleges in operation and maintenance of our physical plant. We are a young institution; we have a plant less than 20 years old. The aging of that plant will make this allocation a future productivity challenge.

More important, however, is the dedication of an able staff. Of eight men and women on our grounds crew, five have been with the university longer than 10 years. This extraordinarily low turnover makes possible higher productivity. Our buildings have been built well, so that we have had few major maintenance problems, such as leaking roofs. The interiors of the buildings were constructed with terrazzo floors and tile hallways, which also account for lower maintenance costs. The plant staff take pride in their work, and the students respect a campus that is kept clean and functional.

This may be a good moment to re-emphasize the point that productivity improvement is more than just a technological challenge. Fifty years have passed since the famous Hawthorne studies conducted at a Western Electric plant by Mayo and colleagues ushered in the human relations movement of American management. In the age of the computer, it may be well to remember that human productivity is directly related to employee recognition and appreciation, to responsibility and involvement. How our colleagues feel about their work and their colleagues is just as important, perhaps more important, than the purchase of a new microcomputer. Effective leaders will be concerned about technology. But they will be concerned first for human caring.

In *The Productivity Challenge*, Michael LeBoeuf indicates that "if productivity gains from 1968 to 1980 had been as high as for the previous ten years, the average U.S. household would have enjoyed almost $4,000 more income in 1980" (p. 7). A closer attention to improved productivity in both administration and instruction may allow us to put more in faculty and staff paychecks. This possible personal benefit may furnish yet another incentive for fresh and imaginative examination of productivity possibilities.

A third incentive can be both personal and artistic. There can be both a private and public pleasure in finding ways to improve efficiency and performance. This pleasure goes beyond that of saving money.

As a 30-year-old registrar, I was also enrolled in a doctoral seminar on industrial psychology in which we studied the major theories of job satisfaction and human motivation, including Maslow's hierarchy-of-needs theory. As I returned from class one day, I was met by my records associate, who advised that one of our filing clerks was resigning and that we needed to complete papers to employ a replacement. This is the linear mind at work. Chancellor or chair, dean or director, the first and most immediate thought when a position is vacated is to file for a quick replacement.

I paused to study this request. What would Maslow have to say about this, I pondered. Who wants to be a filing clerk eight hours a day, when all you have to know is how to count and the alphabet? This is not a job designed to test the higher order needs of humanity. I rejected the request that we hire a replacement and instead suggested that we employ four student workers for two hours a day. These students were pleased to be affiliated in an office at the university, for the opportunity of earning a few dollars and for the privilege of obtaining an early registration permit. They could escape the boredom of the filing task after a couple of hours, and we didn't have to pay staff benefits.

This is a small example, and it did save the university some money; but the real pleasure I derived was not so much from saving the money as seeing an idea work. I know a business executive who, as a general policy, will not allow an immediate replacement. Instead, he tells middle management to wait four to six months before taking any action. He reports that it is surprising how often the business will continue to function without the replacement.

A closing reflection on productivity incentives. One of the reasons public institutions, such as colleges and universities, are not more aggressive about efficiency is that their acts of efficiency often produce a dysfunctional outcome. Money saved is taken from those responsible for the saving and sent elsewhere, whereas in the profit sector those who are responsible for efficiencies can see the competitive posture of their company improving and often receive a direct personal benefit – a trip or a salary bonus.

This note provides a nice bridge to final comments on how education leadership can improve productivity.

The Productivity Promise — A Summary

I like optimists. Stephen Joel Trachtenberg, president of the University of Hartford, is an optimist. He offers a perspective on the past and future of higher education in a commentary titled "Some Good Things Have Come from Hard Times in Academe." Here is his comment about the past:

> Before we romanticize the days of yore and think longingly of the golden years of the 1950s and 1960s, we should remember that a certain slovenliness and lack of control were also characteristic of that time. Money seemed to pour in from every direction. Institutes and special programs multiplied like bacteria in an incredibly rich growth medium. Ideas, even mere hunches, appeared to crystalize in a matter of weeks into full-blown departments equipped with three levels of faculty members, two secretaries, and ten typewriters.

and then. . .

> Demands on the public exchequer, which come from almost every area of American life, are not going to diminish in the future. Where colleges and universities are concerned, things may get a good deal worse financially before they get better. Consequently, we are going to have to make a case for higher education where people can see and hear it, and begin to lobby actively on behalf of our own survival.
>
> . . .I am an optimist, and I feel that we now have an academic structure that is leaner, tougher, and much easier to justify.

As President Trachtenberg notes, one of the primary duties of leadership is to take the case of education before our publics. However, that case must include more than the call for more money. This call will continue to arise from every public service — prisons, transportation, hospitals, welfare. We have the advantage of showing that an investment in education is not just a restorative or preventive function. It is the most constructive long-range investment that a government of the people can make in its future! We must also show that we are effective and efficient stewards of the funds entrusted to our care. For education leaders interested in improving efficiency in the use of resources and in increasing productivity, here are ideas worth remembering.

Ignorance Is Expensive. Leaders who do not know how to motivate, organize, and evaluate, and who remain ignorant of important concepts in human and technical resource management, can deprive their institutions of both effectiveness and efficiency. Good ideas can lead to more efficient application of the resources entrusted to their care.

Duplicity Is Expensive. Leaders who sacrifice their integrity by stealing resources from their institutions are stealing not just from the public but from colleagues, depriving their institutions of efficient management and their colleagues of an improved welfare.

Cowardice Is Expensive. Leaders who know how to improve efficiency but lack the courage to do so are no more effective than the administrator afflicted with managerial ignorance. The result is the same.

Disorganization Is Expensive. Leaders know that organizational style can impede or facilitate talent. Organization is an administrative art form. Dysfunctional arrangements of talent and technology can chew up human and technical resources with no productive outcome, yielding only the destructive heat of tangled personalities, policies, and procedures.

Over-Regulation Is Expensive. Leaders with any sense of artistry know that over-regulation in the management of public funds often produces mismanagement. There is a high cost resulting from mistrust and lack of courage. Control expressed in five-part forms and multiple layers of supervision impedes productivity, as does the lack of courage to deal face to face with offending staff members. The simple device of regular performance and financial audits is more effective than over-regulation.

Disenfranchisement Is Expensive. Education leaders are learning what U.S. business and labor leaders have learned, that all parties have a common stake in improved productivity. And more important, they are learning that a broad reservoir of talent and intelligence is more effective when grappling with productivity issues and in promoting a sense of ownership, which is essential to a healthy organization. The most important incentive for participation in challenges of productivity is the pleasure of being called to responsibility, of sharing in the ownership of the institution's future.

Inefficiency is an enemy of leadership.

References

Abernathy, William J., et al. *Industrial Renaissance*. New York: Basic Books, 1983.

Bulletin of International Economic Conditions. Federal Reserve Bank of St. Louis, June 1984.

Carnegie Commission on Higher Education. *The More Effective Use of Resources: An Imperative for Higher Education*. Berkley, Calif., 1972.

Cyert, Richard. "Carnegie-Mellon Chief Foresees Three-Year Bachelor's Programs." *Chronicle of Higher Education*, 20 June 1984, p. 3.

Harcleroad, Fred F. *Institutionl Efficiency in State Systems of Public Higher Education*. Tucson: Higher Education Program, University of Arizona College of Education, 1975.

Heaton, Herbert. *Productivity in Service Organizations*. New York: McGraw-Hill, 1977.

Increasing Productivity in Higher Education. Princeton, N.J.: Educational Testing Service, 1974.

LeBoeuf, Michael. *The Productivity Challenge*. New York: McGraw-Hill, 1982.

Linowes, David F. "Computers and the Learning Environment." *Vital Speeches of the Day*, 1 May 1984, pp. 439-42.

Lumsden, Keith G., ed. *Efficiency in Universities: The La Paz Papers*. Amsterdam: Elsevier Scientific Publishing Company, 1974.

Maslow, Abraham H. *Motivation and Personality*. New York: Harper & Row, 1954.

National Association of College and University Business Officers/United States Steel Foundation. *1984 Winners of the Cost Reduction Incentive Awards*. Washington, D.C., 1984.

National Center for Education Statistics. *The Condition of Education*. 1984 Edition. Washington, D.C.: U.S. Government Printing Office, 1984.

O'Banion, Terry. "Increasing Productivity in the Community College: A National Effort." *Educational Record* (Spring 1984):42-45.

Sink, D. Scott, et al. "Productivity Measurement and Evaluation: What Is Available?" *National Productivity Review* 3 (Summer 1984):265-87.

Toombs, William. *Productivity: Burden of Success*. ERIC/Higher Education Research Report No. 2. Washington, D.C.: American Association for Higher Education, 1973.

Trachtenberg, Stephen Joel. "Some Good Things Have Come from Hard Times in Academe." *Chronicle of Higher Education*, 23 May 1984, p. 72.

Tucker, Marc S. *Computers on Campus*. Working Papers, Current Issues in Higher Education No. 2. Washington, D.C.: American Association for Higher Education, 1983-84.

Umbeck, Sharvey. "Better Management in Higher Education." *Vital Speeches of the Day*, 1 December 1970, p. 103.

Chapter Nine

The Preservation
of Disorder and Dissent

*The test of a first rate intelligence is the ability to hold two op-
posed ideas in mind at the same time and still retain the ability
to function.*

— F. Scott Fitzgerald

*We do indeed live in an interdependent and process world. We
are both accomplices and colleagues of one another. And I am
not certain this situation is entirely perverse. In the real social-
administrative milieu, with all its complexities, the person who
needs a tidy administration with neat closures and with a cast
of clearly identified villains and heroes will not fare well.*

— Donald Walker
The Effective Administrator

Sometimes silly, sometimes serious, sometimes fascinating, sometimes
frustrating — the world comes to us in contrast and converse, in duality
and dilemma, in polarity and paradox. Reality wears both the mask of come-
dy and tragedy. With the beauty of the rose comes the prick of its thorn.
It is a world of ambiguity.

Let me illustrate the operational meaning of ambiguity with a little story.
It is the tale of the Tennessee truck driver who rounded a curve on Highway 51 north of Memphis with a little too much speed for the pavement,
just dampened by a recent rain. His 18-wheeler jackknifed, threw him
through the windshield, and scattered his load of cattle along a ditch, many
of them bleeding and broken.

Later, he went to court to try to recover some costs for the accident from
his insurance company. The driver was questioned by the company lawyer
as follows: "Sir, will you please tell the court whether or not you admitted

on the evening of the accident that you were not hurt?" The truck driver began to fidget in his seat and sweat poured from his brow, but no answer was forthcoming. The company lawyer pressed the issue: "Yes or no! Did you or did you not admit on the evening of the accident that you were not hurt?"

The truck driver turned with an imploring look to the judge. "Yer Honor," he asked, "Is this here a court of truth, mercy, and justice?"

"Well, yes it is. But what has that got to do with the question?" replied the judge.

"Well, yer honor, I just ain't gonna be able to give yer honor the truth with a yes or no. Could I just have a minute to explain?"

"I suppose so," replied the judge. "But let's be quick about it." The truck driver then told this story. "Yer honor, that there road was a little slick from the rain. And when I rounded the curve, I hit my brakes. And sure nuff, my old truck split. I went one way and my cows went another. A Tennessee state trooper happened to drive up right behind me. He jumped out of his car, ran over and saw my cows bleeding and broken, pulled his Smith and Wesson .38 special, and shot five of my cows right through the head. And then he walked over, with his pistol still smoking, and asked if I was hurt."

With this light-hearted entree to the subject of ambiguity, let us look at management decisions in terms of the options available in leadership style.

- Is the leadership style required one of trust or control?
- Is this a time for reflection or action?
- Is this a moment for participation or power?
- Is the need here for autonomy or accountability?
- Is the remedy appropriate in this situation mercy or justice?
- Is this a moment for confrontation or compromise?
- Is this a service to centralize or decentralize?
- Is the allegiance proper in this case to employee or to organization?
- Is effectiveness to be judged on process or outcome?
- Is the duty here to promote consensus or dissent?

A leader's decisions cannot always advance on the rails of rationality alone. When faced with ambiguous situations, the challenge of leadership is achieving creative balance. Tolerance of ambiguity is a skill of great power in the hands of the artist leader.

Ambiguity in Education Institutions

In *Leadership and Ambiguity: The American College President* (1974), Cohen and March identify four ambiguities facing the contemporary college president. A look at these ambiguities is instructive for all leaders in education institutions.

The Ambiguity of Purpose. The first ambiguity is the difficulty in identifying a clear set of goals for the modern college or university. Cohen and March conclude that "efforts to specify a set of consciously shared, consistent objectives within a university or to infer such a set of objectives from the activities or actions of the university have regularly revealed signs of inconsistency" (p. 196). Their comments are caustic:

> Almost any educated person can deliver a lecture entitled "The Goals of the University." Almost no one will listen to the lecture voluntarily. For the most part, such lectures and their companion essays are well-intentioned exercises in social rhetoric, with little operational content. (p. 195)

Any administrator who has labored to prepare the opening chapter on "Purposes" for a self-study document prior to an accreditation visit can attest to a partial validity in these observations.

Is this, then, the reality of the modern university and its president, a captain and his ship afloat in a sea of uncertainty without a rudder — or even worse, with several hands grasping for control of the helm? How shall we reconcile Cohen and March's comment on inconsistency with Emerson's remark that "A foolish consistency is the hobgoblin of little minds"? And what shall we say about this advice from Keller?

> To have a strategy is to put your own intelligence, foresight, and will in charge instead of outside forces and disordered concerns. (p. 75)

> Defining what business a college is in and then allocating resources to come ahead in that business is tough, intricate, dirty work. (p. 76)

Here we have indeed an ambiguity. A university is both purposeful and serendipitous in its character. Accrediting a college of business will not happen without a sense of purpose and a commitment to operationalize that purpose. Improving the size of campus capital endowment will not occur just by thinking about it. A sense of purpose must energize action to make it happen.

On the other hand, if a benefactor walks into your office, as one did into mine recently, to offer a six-figure endowment for a program of American studies, we do not tell her that such a program is not in our statement of purpose nor in our long-range plan. Universities are collections of purposeful and planned changes, subtle evolutions, and what we Louisianians call "lagniappe," an unexpected good fortune.

The Ambiguity of Power. The picture of the modern university with multiple helmsmen, each struggling to get a hand on the wheel, suggests that the ambiguity of power centers on the office of the president. Cohen and March offer this observation:

> Ambiguity of power leads to a parallel ambiguity of responsibility. The allocation of credit and blame for the events of organizational life

becomes – as it often does in political and social systems – a matter for argument. The "facts" of responsibility are badly confounded by the confusions of anarchy; and the conventional myth of hierarchical executive responsibility is undermined by the countermyth of the non-hierarchical nature of colleges and universities. Presidents negotiate with their audiences on the interpretations of their power. As a result, during the recent years of campus troubles, many college presidents sought to emphasize the limitations of presidential control. During the more glorious days of conspicuous success, they solicited a recognition of their responsibility for events. (p. 198-99)

Not a particularly flattering picture of the presidency. Again, is this the power reality of college leadership? Yes, in part.

There is no question about the diffusion of power and authority on our campuses. Faculty may vote to implement a new program but must yield to the authority of the governing board and perhaps a state coordinating board. The governing board may have legal authority to operate a public university, but the legislature and governor must provide the funds. Personnel actions approved by the board may be tested by the courts. In one state the legislature has prescribed the number of words to be written by students in college composition classes and established a skills test in reading, writing, composition, and essay writing. Students, alumni, and civic and community leadership also have a hand on the university helm.

Is the leader, then, someone who simply sits in the middle of this authority and power net, jostling and posturing when one of the other actors applies some tension? Is this the reality of power in education leadership? Are administrators passive victims of the authority ambiguity in education institutions? Consider the use of power in the following two anecdotes.

Years ago, one of the more daring and colorful department chairmen at a large university took his faculty on a planning retreat – no doubt a worthwhile activity. The problem was that he took them all to New Orleans for the "retreat," which was paid from the public purse. There was some suspicion that eating beignets on the New Orleans riverfront was the prime occupation of this departmental assembly. For some academic vice presidents, this lapse of good judgment would have been a major challenge, a time for investigations and committee hearings. However, this vice president chose a simple and effective approach. He called the chairman in New Orleans and told him to be in the office on Monday morning with a check to cover the full cost of the trip. It was done. The chairman departed at the end of the year. The vice president is still there.

Another academic vice president became irritated because faculty were not being responsible in their fiscal obligations to the university; they were not paying their parking fines. His response was to disapprove the promotion recommended for any faculty member who had not fully paid parking fines due the university. He argued that since students were required to pay such fines before they could receive their diplomas, faculty should do the same. The faculty senate met and voted to "sanction" the vice president. That was 15 years ago. He is still vice president in this university and faculty no longer think twice about whether they should pay parking fines.

These two administrators know about the creative uses of power.

The Ambiguity of Experience. Leaders learn from experience, just as we all do. What we learn affects how we deal with subsequent situations. But experience can also be blinding, causing a leader to make unwarranted inferences from past experience. Cohen and March address this danger in discussing the college presidency:

> College presidents probably have greater confidence in their interpretations of college life, college administration, and their general environment than is warranted. The inferences they have made from experience are likely to be wrong. Their confidence in their learning is likely to have been reinforced by the social support they receive from the people about them and by social expectations about the presidential role. As a result, they tend to be unaware of the extent to which the ambiguities they feel with respect to purpose and power are matched by similar ambiguities with respect to the meaning of the ordinary events of the presidential life. (p. 201)

In view of the ambiguity of experience described by Cohen and March, what kind of leader personality does it take to be able to stand the lonely vigil when convinced that you are right? How will the college president, or any other administrator, know when he or she is right? Must we assume that we are always wrong in our inferences from experience, as suggested by Cohen and March? I think not. Indeed, I see little reason to believe that a leader's learning from experience should be any less valid than another's, especially since the leader may have access to a wider range of information than those operating from a more narrow experience base in the organization. However, Cohen and March's admonition should not go unheeded. Any leader can be blinded to the realities of a situation. He may be arrogant and screen out dissonant feedback. His staff may fear to furnish dissonant feedback.

The Ambiguity of Success. How do leaders judge success – their own and their institutions'? Or should they not even bother but simply preside until someone else does the evaluation? What are the indicators administrators should use to judge success – growth, mobility, involvement, activity, power, salary? Cohen and March make this despairing comment about judging the success of college presidents:

> The result is that the president is a bit like the driver of a skidding automobile. The marginal judgments he makes, his skill, and his luck, may possibly make some difference to the survival prospects for his

riders. As a result, his responsibilities are heavy. But whether he is convicted of manslaughter or receives a medal for heroism is largely outside his control. (p. 203)

For the college president who reads this passage at the end of a long and difficult day, the tendency might simply be to take his hands off the wheel, let the university car skid in whatever direction it decides to move, and let fate work its own end.

In Cohen and March's book, we are given a pessimistic perspective on the theme of administrative ambiguity. For contrast, let us consult some sources that take a more optimistic look at ambiguity.

Peters and Waterman in their study of America's best-run companies identified eight variables that discriminate these companies from others. One of the eight is the quality of ambiguity. These companies have what Peters and Waterman describe as "simultaneous loose-tight properties." The same phrase has been picked up in a recent *National Center for Higher Education Management Systems Newsletter* (June 1984):

> The most effective institutions are those with both loose and tight coupling, stability and flexibility, centralization and broad participation. Effective administrators will manage these paradoxes, not try to eliminate them. (p. 17)

In his provocative volume, *Servant Leadership* (1977), Robert K. Greenleaf identifies three ambiguities in modern organizations. First is the "operational necessity to be both dogmatic and open to change." Most organizations need the force of policy and precedent for orderly movement but also need to depart from or make exceptions to policy in order to survive. A second ambiguity is the "disability that goes with competence." Competence usually increases with specialization, but the more specialized we become the more narrow our vision can be. And when the challenge of change in the environment affects organizational mission or resources, narrowness of vision does not always serve an organization well. The third ambiguity is the need for a "healthy tension between belief and criticism." Here Greenleaf suggests a role distinction between administrators and their staffs and that of organizational trustees. Greenleaf explains:

> Administrators and staffs need to be mostly believing because the morale of those who do the work of the institution needs to be sustained, and part of the trust of all constituencies rests on a communicated belief in the rightness of what is being done.
>
> Trustees need to be mostly critical because it is the scrutiny of a critical attitude that keeps administrators and staff on a true course. (p. 106)

What may we learn from this examination of ambiguity in organizations? Is it only possible to suggest that the administrator "hang loose"? No. In the disorder and dissent that are characteristic of ambiguity reside the genesis of more effective programs, policies, and practices that can strengthen an organization.

The Uses of Ambiguity

I have presented the several faces of ambiguity in institutions and organizations. In this section we shall look more closely at the kinds of ambiguity leaders face and see how these can be used to create more effective leadership.

Look for Power and Promise in Ambiguous Situations. Dilemma — a challenge of two unsatisfactory choices. Here is a 30-year-old assistant professor of history up for tenure review. If this candidate is tenured, the history department will be 100% tenured, a position that potentially limits the vitality of the department. To deny tenure would prevent the department from retaining a promising talent. Is there a third way?

The dean of faculty is confronted by a 40-year-old construction foreman angry over a "D" received in a marketing course. He claims that the grade he received is not because of his lack of knowledge of the course content but because his papers were not typed, as the instructor required. A faculty appeals committee reviews the academic suspension as a result of this grade but offers no exception to the instructor's policy. To overrule the committee could result in the dean being charged with lowering academic standards and with interfering with a faculty prerogative. To sustain the committee's ruling could be devastating to the motivation of this serious older student. Was his grade and subsequent academic suspension justified on the basis of whether his papers were typed? Is there a third way?

Perhaps the history assistant professor can be appointed to a multi-year contract. Even if the construction foreman's suspension is upheld, perhaps his motivation could be sustained by allowing him to enroll for audit the next term. It pays to ask whether decision dilemmas are truly dichotomous or whether there is a third way.

Duality — two opposing principles at work, each a face of reality. Can weakness beget strength? A college dean — known for his strength of personality as well as physique, possessed with an aggressive drive for goal setting and planning, obsessed by rationality and punctuality — is struck down by cancer on his way up the collegiate executive ladder. He is knocked flat on his back for a long period and is forced to think about himself, his values, and what is important in life. He conquers the cancer and emerges a man whose basic personality and drive are still intact. But he is a man softened and sensitized to other realities in life, a man who now goes to his office each day with a thought not only for the to-do list on his memo pad but also for the secretaries and the faculty colleagues for whom he is responsible. He is now an executive vice president, with a capacity for compassion that he did not seem to have before his forced introspection.

Paradox — a statement seemingly opposed to common sense, yet true. Here is a small mystery. Why can I spend days thinking about the content and organization of this chapter and toss about as I attempt to go to sleep trying to arrive at a framework for what I want to say? But not until I actually sit down to the typewriter and start to write does the outline of the chapter evolve. An idea intended for closing is shoved to the lead paragraph, a quotation hiding in a book on the library shelf arrives unannounced, an illustration pops into mind on the drive to the Rotary Club. The conventional wisdom is that one outlines and then one writes. But in reality, out of the act of writing comes the organization; one informs the other. I must be willing to write without having full closure.

Complementarity — two opposite but mutually supporting principles. The new chairman of the faculty senate struggles to define his "authority." Although he presides over the collegial body of university authority, he has no veto or other executive option as the chief officer of the senate. On the other hand, the president of the university can veto any action of the faculty senate, according to the university bylaws, but he cannot start new courses nor change admissions requirements by unilateral action. These two forms of authority — one collegial and the other hierarchical — are in a complementary tension. It is both discomforting and exciting.

Ambiguity — statements capable of different but equally acceptable meanings. Is the contemporary American university servant or critic? Perhaps both. Is the structure of the modern American university hierarchical or collegial? Perhaps both. Is the authority structure of the American university consultative and consensual or authoritarian and directive? Perhaps both. Is the success of the American university to be measured in the short-range knowledge and skill achievements of its graduates or in their long-range achievements? Perhaps both. Who is really in charge of the public university — the faculty, the president, the governing board, the legislature, the governor? Perhaps all of them. Are we to organize the university around functional or task lines? Can we have both permanent and temporary structures, bureaucracy and "adhocracy," at work at the same time? Perhaps so.

The foregoing has presented the contrasting faces of leadership from my perspective as a college administrator. What other lessons can we learn?

Resist Temptation for Quick Closure. In my earlier days as an academic administrator, I had a great proclivity for order. There had to be a category and a policy for everything. The neater the organizational chart the better I felt. I characterized myself as having a great love for organization and order. My friends called it rigidity. In more recent years, I have been learning to live a little more comfortably with disorder. I have learned that it does not always pay to rush in and close on a problem, that occasionally it may be better to let matters percolate a bit, that quick closure is sometimes the cause of other problems.

I receive an angry and arrogant letter from a local attorney. It concerns a student who has been academically suspended and has appealed that suspension, but whose appeal is denied by the faculty-student appeals committee. The attorney "demands" to know the reasons and "requires" that I respond within 10 days. I am furious.

Issuing fire and smoke from every cranial opening, I compose a letter that fairly sizzles. I remind the attorney that she is just an attorney and not a judge. And I tell her that I do not operate on her 10-day time frame. I suggest that if she learns to write without such pomposity and arrogance of tone she will become more effective. This is all very cathartic for me and also gives me a good sense of closure.

Do I send the letter? I am sorely tempted because such arrogance needs a good stiff rebuttal. But I consider the matter overnight. In the morning, I call the university legal counsel and request his advice concerning my sending this hot missile. He laughs, sympathizes, and then suggests a cooler response. His suggested approach does not provide me with the closure or catharsis I sought, but it does dispatch the issue without any ragged or expensive follow-up.

One should not conclude from these remarks that I think administrators should not occasionally compose hotly worded letters or memos. To the contrary, the *writing* of such communications often serves as a therapeutic release. It is the *sending* of the letters where I counsel caution. If in doubt about the impact of an "impulse" communication, test its content and tone on a trusted colleague or let it sit on your desk for a day or so before sending it. Keep all those that you decide not to send in a personal folder and look at them from time to time to remind yourself of how much trouble you could have created if you had sent them.

Actively Promote Some Dissent. In *The Future Executive*, Harland Cleveland suggested that the wise executive would promote "enough loud and cheerful argument among [staff] members so that all possible outcomes are analyzed.... the moral dilemmas are illuminated, and the public effects are analytically examined" (p. 22). Tension reduction is a powerful human inclination. To resolve conflict, to relieve stress, to reduce tension are natural impulses. It is, therefore, a discomforting notion to think about doing just the opposite. However, some amount of deliberately promoted dissent and disorder can stimulate both thought and action.

Here are the dean of students and the dean of business in a discussion on the coordination and management of student internships. The argument is a lively one, just as Cleveland recommends. Though a little strained, it remains cheerful as well. The dean of students insists that the university is not large enough to justify or afford internship coordinators in each of the colleges and that this should be a student service operating out of his division. He further maintains that internship coordination has a natural and functional alliance with placement, which he already operates. The dean of business takes the position that a single person cannot possibly have the breadth of contact and experience to arrange internships across the many disciplines of the university. Besides, he points out, the College of Education devotes half a faculty position to coordination of its student teaching program. Why should the College of Business be denied a like opportunity? Both want a decision from the executive vice president today. Here are two leadership bugaboos at work again – the press for decision closure and the press of a decision dichotomy. The executive vice president decides to let the issue rest for a few days, with no apparent damage that she can ascertain. She finally decides to let some internship coordination develop in both places, just to see how it will work out and what relationships will emerge.

Although administrators need not keep the organizational stew in a constant stir, they can make artistic use of dissent, knowing that a touch of ambiguity can make us stand on our intellectual tip-toes.

Develop Multiple Management Approaches. American management culture tends to reinforce a macho, head-on approach to management issues. We have a "High Noon" mentality, a confrontational set, where the good guy and the bad guy meet in the dusty street. American management culture also values strength of personality and decisiveness in the face of adversity. Now there is nothing inherently wrong in this heroic frame of reference; but there are times and places when a good question becomes a softer, longer lasting influence for personnel and program change than the giving of orders and pronouncements. Questions and suggestions, going with the flow, let colleagues have an opportunity to save face, to develop ownership in ideas. An Eastern thought suggests that we should persist like the stream, whose patient and continual flow will eventually wear away any rigid barrier.

A dean of a performing arts college is unhappy with the performance standards of her drama program. After attending the drama productions of area high schools, she comes to the conclusion that most of the college drama presentations do not match the artistic and performing standards of these high schools. This not only is inconsistent with the college's strong academic reputation in other areas, but it makes it difficult to attract good high school students to enroll in the college drama program.

She suspects the source of difficulty lies with the quality of the director of theater. But how to bring about a qualitative change is the challenge. Under conventional management principles, the dean might deliver a bill of particulars to the director or drama faculty. After all, a straight-from-the-heart, honest, open approach to the problem will clear the air. This is the sledgehammer approach so often favored in American management.

Quite as powerful in its long-term impact, however, is the force of subtlety. Perhaps inviting the director and faculty to accompany her to review local high school plays would serve a dual prupose — to show the college's interest in area high schools and to give these drama department colleagues a chance to ask questions about performance standards. A gentle question inserted here and there in the coffee lounge or over lunch may come to rest on fertile ground.

There is other merit in this more gentle and patient approach. The dean may find that she is part of the problem, a finding she most certainly would not discover if she had just fired her evaluative cannon at the director and faculty. For example, to what extent do the college facilities and financial support match those of the high schools? Has the dean failed in her inspirational and support role? A change in our management frame of reference permits us to discover that problem identification and resolution is a team affair.

Does this mean that the heroic model of leadership is out? Passé? No! It means that we should keep both the heroic and the more subtle frames of reference in mind at the same time. We are leadership artists, not automatons.

Cultivate a Hospitality to Error and Dissent. In a delightful little book, *The Medusa and the Snail*, physician-author Lewis Thomas says:

> If we were not provided with the knack of being wrong, we could never get anything useful done. . . . the capacity to leap across mountains of information to land lightly on the wrong side represents the highest of human endowments. (p. 37-39)

The history of much human progress is the serendipitous outcomes of error. The artist administrator is hospitable to this idea. Furthermore, hospitality to error makes one more patient with imperfection and mistakes.

A hospitality to dissent keeps the administrator from the destructive tendency of assuming pathological motives on the part of those with whom he may disagree. It also keeps the leader from what Daniel Boorstin has called the "illusion of knowledge." In *The Discoverers* (1983), Boorstin describes the interaction of science and religion and makes the point that the most significant impediment to man's advancement of new ideas is not his ignorance but the illusion of knowledge. Here is his explanation.

Copernicus was described as an "upstart astrologer" by Martin Luther, who said of Copernicus, "This fool wishes to reverse the entire science of astronomy; but sacred scriptures tell us that Joshua commanded the sun to stand still, and not the earth." Here is a man who created a revolution in religious thought casting verbal stones at one who created a revolution in our view of the universe. And Luther did so because he believed he had a lock on knowledge. What he really had was the "illusion of knowledge."

135

Administrators need the force of dissent to keep them from both arrogance and the illusion of knowledge. They need to test the validity of their ideas in the hot crucible of experience in competition with the ideas of others. It may be more comfortable to work with sycophants rather than with colleagues who are occasionally insolent, egocentric, argumentative, and critical; but we need about us stalwart spirits, quick minds, and courageous hearts.

Leaders who wish to improve their own effectiveness and that of their institutions will not only tolerate dissent and disorder, they will occasionally foster it. They will be known not just for the problems they have solved but also for the problems they have uncovered. They will not be spared the discomfort of ambiguity but rather will use ambiguity creatively to achieve constructive balance in decisions, organization, authority, and evaluation.

Rigidity is an enemy of leadership.

References

Boorstin, Daniel J. *The Discoverers*. New York: Random House, 1983.

Cleveland, Harlan. *The Future Executive*. New York: Harper & Row, 1972.

Cohen, Michael D., and March, James G. *Leadership and Ambiguity: The American College President*. New York: McGraw-Hill, 1974.

Davies, Richard. "Creative Ambiguity." *Religious Education* 77 (November-December 1982): 642-56.

Emerson, Ralph. "Self Reliance." In *The Complete Writings of Ralph Waldo Emerson*. New York: William H. Wise and Company, 1929.

Greenleaf, Robert K. *Servant Leadership*. New York: Paulist Press, 1977.

Keller, George. *Academic Strategy: The Management Revolution in American Higher Education*. Baltimore: Johns Hopkins University Press, 1983.

"Organizational Effectiveness in Higher Education." *National Center for Higher Education Management Systems Newsletter*, June 1984, p. 7.

Peters, Thomas J., and Waterman, Jr., Robert H. *In Search of Excellence*. New York: Harper & Row, 1972.

Thomas, Lewis. *The Medusa and the Snail*. New York: Viking, 1974.

Chapter Ten
_____

The Low Road to Morality

*The really serious matters of life cannot be calculated. We can-
not directly calculate what is right but we jolly well know what
is wrong.*

— Ernest Schumacher
Small Is Beautiful

*[M]oral and spiritual progress is infinitely more difficult than
technological progress; . . . even surrounded and served by in-
tricate and marvelous machines, man may be little more than
a cruel and clever ape — unless he constantly thinks about what
is truly good and strives to attain it.*

— Gilbert Highet
The Immortal Profession

In Sophocle's tragedy *Antigone*, King Kreon observes that it is hard to
learn the mind or heart of a man until he is tried in authority and power.
The moral fibre of men and women in leadership positions is tested daily
in actions of authority and power. I began this book with the proposition
that many leaders fail in their promise and bring their institutions in harm's
way not so much by lack of technical skill as by the sacrifice of their integrity. I conclude with this same theme.

It is troubling to pick up the morning newspaper or tune to the evening
news to learn of physicians forsaking their integrity by ripping off the Medi-
care system, of lawyers breaking the law they are sworn to uphold by helping prisoners escape, of military officers abandoning their commission oath
by trading defense secrets, of airline executives stealing from their company even while it is going into bankruptcy, of bankers misappropriating funds
for their private use, of politicians betraying the public trust with kickback
deals. These acts destroy our trust and lead us to suspicion and cynicism.
Each act weakens the foundation of a democratic society.

It is a pleasant and comfortable vision that our colleges and universities are immune from the black marks of wrongdoing, that we are dutifully going about the business of equipping our graduates for noble and ethical service in society as they leave our portals. There are, regrettably, dirty smears in that vision.

The Moral Context in Education Institutions

Consider the incident of a dozen athletes from a university taking a summer course in a community college, which is designed to keep them eligible for the coming season. These hearty fellows are enrolled in a three-hour course that amounts to riding a yellow school bus and touring the athletic departments of several local school systems. This is a pitiful excuse for what is supposed to be college-level work. College leaders who might have prevented such nonsense are too busy negotiating TV contracts.

Reports of ethical breaches ride the waves of modern communication and break on distant shores. I can read of a college president who has plagiarized his dissertation, a student affairs vice president who has purchased his doctoral degree from a shadowy institution whose only capital asset is the letterhead of its stationery. A college recruiting officer pays his high school relations officers a "bounty" for recruiting certain kinds of students. A cell of undergraduate accounting students, graduate assistants, and one professor is found operating a test-cheating ring. This scheme is not designed to help weak students but rather to help good students turn a "B" into an "A" so that they will look better to Peat Marwick and Mitchell on graduation.

A few years ago, I was invited to Washington, along with many other college presidents, to participate in a workshop on federal legislation affecting higher education. One hot topic of concern was the future federal funding level for student aid. At the conclusion of the workshop we were asked to visit our representatives and senators to lobby their support for maintenance and, if possible, increases in federal student aid programs. Appointments had been arranged in advance for this purpose.

On the way to the Shreveport Regional Airport the morning of my flight to Washington, I turned on the car radio and heard this disturbing story. Who do you suppose was in loan default to the federal government for more than $700 million dollars? Lockheed or Chrysler, perhaps? No. Those owing the federal government were graduates of our colleges and universities – physicians, teachers, accountants, historians, engineers who had defaulted on federal loan accounts.

This was a difficult matter for me. I had grown up with the simple ethic that if you borrowed money, you paid it back. As an undergraduate in the 1950s I had borrowed money from my church, my brother, and the small bank in my home town. Later as a doctoral student I was grateful for an NDEA loan. I paid these loans back.

139

How could I ask senators and representatives to support increases in student aid when some colleges and universities were not being responsible in collecting funds already allocated? In fact, some institutions even advanced the twisted notion that these loans were more in the form of a grant than a loan — a notion that was not lost on students.

That ethical issues are of crucial contemporary interest to collegiate leadership is clear to anyone who looks at the current literature. In 1979, concerned over the rights and responsibilities of students and their colleges in a period of intensified competition for enrollments, the Carnegie Council on Policy Studies in Higher Education published *Fair Practices in Higher Education*. In 1980 the Hastings Center published a major report and a book supplement titled *Ethics Teaching in Higher Education*. In 1981 Jossey-Bass published *Professional Ethics in University Administration*. In recent years two of higher education's most respected journals, *The Educational Record* (Spring 1984) and *The Journal of Higher Education* (May-June 1982), devoted whole issues to ethics in colleges and universities. The journal *Change* had earlier carried articles on ethics (see Callahan and Bok 1979).

There are two important lessons that we can learn from these books, journals, and reports. One of them has been identified by David Dill in his critique of *Ethics Teaching in Higher Education*. Dill lists the curricular options for the teaching of ethics: issue-oriented courses, professional ethics courses, traditional philosophy and moral reasoning courses. He then observes that "the behavior of the individual faculty member does not explicitly appear in this list. That it does not, that small influence is attributed to faculty conduct, is, I would submit, a characteristic value of the academic profession" (p. 247). A professor teaching a course in ethics for the medical, business, legal, or teaching profession, who fails to model ethical behavior in his own life and in the conduct of the course itself, is teaching a sorry lesson.

A second lesson is found in a critique of ethics teaching by William J. Bennett, writing in *Commentary* (December 1980). Reading *Ethics Teaching in Higher Education* and some of the journal pieces reveals that much of what has been written is ethically neutral, leaving the impression that Barbara Tuchman describes as: "Everyone is afraid to call anything wrong, or vulgar, or fraudulent, or just bad taste or bad manners" (p. 3). Here is what Bennett has to say about one of the programs described in *Ethics Teaching in Higher Education*:

> A program of moral education like this one leaves ethical matters just where the moral cynic wants them — perpetually suspended in debate, in controversy, in "wrestling." By the terms of this program, he can insist on tolerance from others for his point of view, pointing out that he merely reflects the values "of a different ethical strand in society." (p. 64.)

Why are we so inclined to timidity when it comes to imposing our values on others? Perhaps it is because we know from history how many good minds and lives have been cruelly sacrificed for daring to hold ideas and values that were at variance with prevailing opinion. The breastplate of righteousness requires a stalwart bearer when recommending values for others. One cannot expect to venture into ethical advocacy without challenge. Should you doubt this, consider the following examples of clashes in values.

In an interview carried in *U.S. News and World Report* (21 February 1983), Derek Bok, president of Harvard University, discusses the need for students to grapple with significant ethical problems but offers the following caution:

> But efforts by universities to teach students about ethical issues are likely to be limited in value and to produce cynicism if the institutions themselves are perceived to be ethically careless or insensitive. That doesn't mean we have to agree with the students or take institutional positions on public questions of the day, which I think would be wrong. (p. 83)

Now consider the value conflict posed by conservative columnist William Buckley in the *Shreveport Times* (8 August 1984) in which he takes on President Bok and Harvard on the issue of an avowed communist holding appointment as chairman of the History Department. Buckley quotes Bok as saying, "The fact that he is a communist is not, of itself, a matter of concern to us so long as he does not seek to indoctrinate his students." To which Buckley comments:

> It is the very beginning of political wisdom to recognize that affiliation with some political movements is not primarily a political act — it is a moral commitment, or rather, an extramoral commitment. There is no such thing as a Nazi who is also qualified to teach in a community of scholars. Nor is there such a thing as a communist qualified to teach in a community of scholars. The only thing more anesthetizing to moral sensibilities than to have a communist on a faculty of a college is to have as its president someone who cannot penetrate that distinction. (p. 5B)

We are not through. A few days later in the "Letters to the Editor" appears an attack on Buckley's column that concludes, "That the usually compelling Buckley presents so unsound an argument in this particular column is not so disturbing. What is disturbing is that the column's level of self-righteousness is so directly proportional to the complacency of its rhetoric" (Cush 1984).

So much, then, for the comfort of those who dare to stand for anything. All of us are caught up each day by ethical challenges, some trivial, others of more serious import. Only when our values are challenged are we tested on how secure they are.

Moral Cognition

According to *Ethics Teaching in Higher Education*, the role of the college president in the teaching of ethics was at one time a highly active one for at least one institution:

> In 1895, the Amherst College catalogue devoted the entire front page of the section on "The Course of Study" to a description of the course in ethics taught by the president of the college to the senior class. (p. 9)

What better way for the president to be a model than to teach ethics to undergraduates. Chairman or chancellor, registrar or dean, whether in front of a class or not, is still teaching lessons in ethics:

> Do I make an exception to the retention policy and readmit the son of the board chairman?

> Do I place university financial accounts with a certain local bank so that I can gain a private, no-interest loan in exchange?

> Do I overlook the probability of a changed grade on a student's high school transcript so that I can obtain a complimentary set of tickets to the football and basketball season?

> Do I ignore the fact that several accounting faculty are cutting short office hours during tax season so they can earn extra income preparing tax returns?

> Do I reprimand the professor of marketing for using university computer facilities to analyze results on questionnaires being used in private consulting work?

What is the ethical duty of the college president? Here are visions from two men who have served in that role. Donald Walker says:

> The president's task as ethical leader is not to try to achieve academic sainthood; it is his or her task to provide healing interpretations to the academic community.... It is the president's job to mediate and arrive at creative solutions. It is the job of the president to create an environment where dialectical change is encouraged, where people deal with one another not as scoundrels but as colleagues, and where different interests and perspectives may be compromised in ways that resolve tension and permit action. (pp. 26-27)

Harold Enarson offers this view:

> To lead the college or the university is to transform it over time so that it better reflects the finest values of society, thus offering splendid service to the highest human aspirations. (p. 25)

What are those "highest human aspirations?" Before making a more specific point of ethical advocacy, let me discuss briefly the issue of means and ends in matters of values, just to remind ourselves that resolving ethical issues is not a matter of applying a simple recipe.

Psychologist Milton Rokeach, in *The Nature of Human Values* (1973), suggests that our values can be clustered in two sets, instrumental and terminal — values of means and values of ends. In reflecting on the ethical implications of his research, Rokeach asks:

> Is it ever permissible, in the scientific laboratory, in the classroom, or in the real world, to enduringly change other people without their fully informed consent? (p. 335)

And then he observes:

> every teacher who takes professional pride in his work would like to think that his teaching has affected the values, attitudes, and behavior of his students in some significant way. (p. 335)

Healthy or pathological, our values do indeed leave a mark. We are, willing or not, models to whom others look for operational definitions of values of means and values of ends.

Aristotle, Augustine, and Aquinas are some of our great ethical thinkers whose names begin with *A*. My own ethical thinking has been influenced by a more contemporary writer whose last name also begins with an *A*. While his writings may not be included in the classical ethical literature, I find him immensely provocative. I refer to Saul Alinsky and his book, *Rules for Radicals*. Alinsky opens his chapter titled "Of Means and Ends" with this note.

> The men who pile up heaps of discussion and literature on the ethics of means and ends — which with rare exception is conspicuous for its sterility — rarely write about their own experiences in the perpetual struggle of life and change. (p. 25)

He then poses a set of rules related to the ethics of means and ends. Here they are paraphrased:

1. *One's concern with the ethics of means and ends varies inversely with one's personal interest in the issue.* In other words, the further we are from being involved in the conflict, the more interested we tend to be in the means-end question. We are parlor philosophers.
2. *The judgment of the ethics of means is dependent on the political position of those sitting in judgment.* If, for example, you thought the Nazi occupation of France in World War II a dastardly act, then partisan acts of assassination, terror, property destruction, kidnapping, and other means of resistance were not so bad.
3. *In war, the end justifies almost any means.* Winston Churchill once indicated that he had only one purpose, to defeat Hitler, and that if Hitler were to invade Hell, he would make at least a favorable reference to the Devil in the House of Commons.

4. *Judgment must be made in the context of the times in which the action occurred and not from any other chronological vantage point.* How do we contrast our position on freedom of the high seas in 1812 and 1917 compared with our blockade of Cuba in 1962?

5. *Concern with ethics increases with the number of means available and vice versa.* If there is only one means available, then the ethical question of means will never arise. "What else could I do?"

6. *The less important the end to be desired, the more one can afford to engage in ethical evaluations of the means.*

7. *Success or failure is a mighty determinant of ethics.* There can be no such thing as a successful traitor, for if one succeeds, one becomes a founding father.

8. *The morality of a means depends on whether the means is being employed at a time of imminent defeat or imminent victory.* If the atomic bomb had been dropped on Japan immediately following Pearl Harbor, there would have been little conflict over that means.

9. *An effective means is automatically judged by the opposition as being unethical.* In the Revolutionary War, the British labeled Francis Marion, the "Swamp Fox," as a criminal and charged that he did not engage in warfare like a gentleman or Christian. There is now a college in South Carolina named for this revolutionary.

10. *You do what you can with what you have and clothe it in moral arguments.* Mahatma Gandhi's use of passive resistance is a good example of time working on the ethics of means and ends. When the position of the have-nots changes to that of the haves, then there is a change of goals from getting to keeping.

Alinsky concludes that the true ethical question is, "Does this particular end justify this particular means?"

Alinsky has a humorous style, but I suspect he is not so humorous to experience. Among the guidelines he suggests for agents of change is that you work with what you have and you stay legal. Invited to Rochester, New York, by minorities who had been unsuccessful in getting city leadership to deal with housing and other complaints, Alinsky was faced with how to stay within this guideline and get the attention of the city fathers.

Now Rochester is the home of the Eastman School of Music and a symphony orchestra of which the city is very proud. Here is what Alinsky counseled:

> I suggested that we might buy one hundred seats for one of Rochester's symphony concerts. We would select a concert in which the music was relatively quiet. The hundred blacks who would be given the tickets would first be treated to a three-hour pre-concert dinner in the community, in which they would be fed nothing but baked beans, and lots

of them. Then the people would go to the symphony hall — with obvious consequences. Imagine the scene when the action began! The concert would be over before the first movement! (p. 139)

And what could the authorities do, Alinsky asked:

> Demand that people not eat baked beans before coming to a concert? Ban anyone from succumbing to natural urges during the concert? (p. 140)

Any person with a sense of humor cannot read these passages without at least a snicker; but if you had been in attendance at this concert, it might not have been very humorous.

Here is one of the major ethical propositions of Alinsky's book:

> I believe that man is about to learn that the most practical life is the moral life and that the moral life is the only road to survival. He is beginning to learn that he will either share part of his material wealth or lose all of it; that he will respect and learn to live with other political ideologies, if he wants civilization to go on. This is the kind of argument that man's actual experience equips him to understand and to accept. This is the low road to morality. There is no other. (p. 23)

There is another road about which I shall say more in a moment.

Another lively and contemporary treatise on an ethical topic is Sissela Bok's book *Lying* (1979). Here are some of the questions posed by Bok:

1. Since many believe that we can never know the whole truth about anything, does it matter whether or not we lie if we have a good reason to do so?
2. But what does the prevalence of deceit do to the order of trust in our society? And what does it do to liars themselves?
3. Can we subscribe to the proposition of some theologians and religious scholars that lying is never justified under any circumstances?
4. If not, then what are the tests and principles that may be applied?

Bok then leads us to reflect on these questions: Do you tell a "white lie" when your wife asks your opinion about her new clothes? Do you offer an "excuse" when you are asked to a social event on the one night you had planned to be with your family? If a Nazi stormtrooper shows up at your door and asks if you are harboring a Jew, do you tell a lie in a crisis to protect a life? If a professional colleague is guilty of malpractice, do you tell a lie to protect a peer? Do you tell a lie in the conduct of research for the purpose of advancing knowledge? Do you tell a lie to an ill or dying patient?

Bok goes beyond the posing of these questions. She applies three principles to justify the telling of a lie:

we must ask, first, whether there are alternative forms of action which will resolve the difficulty without the use of a lie; second, what might be the moral reasons brought forward to excuse the lie, and what reasons can be raised as counter arguments. Third, as a test of these two steps, we must ask what a public of reasonable persons might say about such lies. (pp. 111-12)

It is this final test — the test of public review — that I want to stress in concluding this discussion.

Moral Commitment

Throughout this book I have emphasized the linking of thought with action. Ethical commitment does not come from reading essays on ethics, nor from writing them. Without the test of action and decision we are moral pedants whose lessons will be sterile and empty. To see ethical decision making in action, I use the incident told in *The Ultra Secret* (Winterbotham 1974) about how the German machine cypher code in World War II was broken, which provided critical intelligence information to Churchill, Roosevelt, and other allied leaders.

On 14 November 1941 the Allies received a piece of intelligence that would test the ethical fiber of the most stalwart leaders. According to the Ultra intelligence sources, the Germans planned a bombing raid on Coventry. To alert the citizens of Coventry would signal to the Germans that the British had foreknowledge of the raid and thus put in jeopardy the Ultra operation. Civic panic and a consequent higher loss of life was also a possibility. Churchill and his advisors decided against the full civic alert and instead alerted only fire fighters, police, and service units. The local officials arranged for the lighting of decoy fires to confuse the bombers.

Leaders may have strong moral commitment but still find themselves thrust into agonizing ethical dilemmas where the right course of action is uncertain, where rules are unavailable, where computers are silent, where staff can advise but only the leader can decide. A physician knows the utilitarian ethic. Will he let one terminally ill patient die so that he can use the organs that might save four other patients? What of the general who orders a unit into battle in the face of damaging odds, knowing that his son is a member of that unit? What of the accountant who discovers that his client has engaged in illegal acts and has others planned? What of the teacher who must weigh the future welfare of a student against standards required in an education institution? What of an engineer who is asked to falsify data to ensure the acceptance of a company product?

In the novel *Daughter of Silence* (1961) by Morris West, the character Rienzi is testifying before a court on the relationship between law and justice. His testimony is instructive:

Mr. President, gentlemen of the court.... My learned friend has spoken to you of the law. To hear him, you would believe that the law is something fixed, immutable, beyond dispute or interpretation. This is not so. The law is a body of traditions, precedents and ordinances: some good, some bad, but all dedicated in principle, if not in fact, to the security of the subject, the maintenance of public order and the dispensation of moral justice. Sometimes these ends accord with one another. Sometimes they are in contradiction; so that justice may be ill-served while order is most securely maintained. Sometimes the ordinance is too simple, sometimes it is too detailed; so that there is always need for gloss and annotation and the conflict of opinions to arrive at its true intent. The Decalogue says, bluntly: "Thou shalt not kill." Is this the end of it? You know it is not. You put a uniform on a man's back and a gun in his hands and you say, "It is a holy and blessed thing to kill for one's country." And you pin a medal on his chest when he does it.... Let us be clear on this issue, gentlemen. The law is an instrument and not an end. It is not, and never can be, a perfect instrument of justice. (p. 199)

I spoke of ambiguity in the previous chapter. Here Rienzi shows us the ambiguity in law. Leadership integrity cannot be found in a set of rules, a program flowchart. Nor can leadership be found in the ethical neutrality of some moral marshmallow who offers no resistance to wrongdoing.

There is no single road to justice and morality. There is a low road to morality, as described by Alinsky. We do what is right because we fear an audit that will check on our actions. We do what is right because we fear the reprisal of those whom we may cheat. But there is a high road to morality as well. We do what is right because we care about both principle and people. We do what is right because we have compassion.

Now the question of compassion among administrators is not a simple issue. Organizational scholar Victor Thompson has written provocatively about this issue in *Without Sympathy or Enthusiasm: The Problem of Administrative Compassion* (1975). His major thematic question in the book is:

Can modern organizations be compassionate? Can they "care"? Can organizations be depicted as good or bad, kind or cruel? From everything we know about modern organizations, the answer has to be "No!" (p. 8)

Thompson answers his question with this statement, "In the final analysis, compassion is an individual gift, not an organizational one" (p. 13).

Thompson sees the problem of compassion in organizations and among administrators as a difficult one because:

To recognize another claim is to "steal" the owner's property.... The goal of a public welfare organization, for example, is what the "public" wants for recipients of welfare, not what the welfare recipients want for themselves. (p. 10)

147

How do we react to Thompson's statement that administrative compassion may mean "stealing" from the organization's owners? Our reaction to an organization can be both technical and personal. I may find it pleasurable to fly an L-1011 with Delta Airlines. However, if the ticket agent or flight attendant is rude, then the technical splendor of the aircraft may not compensate. On the other hand, if one of those L-1011 engines quits in mid-air, then I am interested in survival not courtesy. The repairman at Sears may be cordial; but if my Weedwacker grass trimmer keeps breaking down every week, then service cordiality will not compensate for the product failure.

Ultimately, the technical and service faces of any organization are human resource challenges. The leader who fails to promote both product and service excellence from the men and women who give life to an organization may not have stolen from the organization, but he will have produced a similar result — loss of reputation, loss of business. The difference is in the intent, not in the result. Let me illustrate.

The director of finance for a large university has an administrative style that is stifling. He practices heavy-breathing supervision, regularly berates erring accountants in front of other employees, and spreads fear of mistakes among his staff. He accords his staff little dignity nor independence. As a result he attracts only small-spirited people to work in this climate. The turnover rate in this office is three times that of any other office on campus. The return on university invested dollars is far below other schools with similar resources. Is he stealing from the university? It may not be charitable, or even accurate, to use that term, but he is certainly depriving the organization of reputation and performance, of maximum use of both its technical and human resources.

Consider the disposition of a college registrar who believes that she is being compassionate when she is sitting one-on-one with a student with a problem. She derives personal satisfaction in helping resolve student problems, but the fact that several hundred students are waiting in line because her registration process has become unraveled she does not see as a problem. And so with her friendly disposition she resides comfortably in a nest of worn-out procedures, outdated forms, contradictory policies, and fails to see that these may be why she is seeing so many students one-on-one. Ensuring the efficiency of her technical functions related to the registration process is also an act of caring — an act of compassion.

There are acts of administrative compassion that take nothing from an organization's resources but add to its strength. Let me share a personal example.

When I was in upper elementary school, I decided that I wanted to play in the school band. I started out playing the E-flat mellophone, graduating later to the French horn. To this day, I remember what at the time seemed a terrible day in the sixth grade. Tucked away in a room under the gym bleacher seats at Millington Central School, our small band was struggling with that difficult work "Little Primrose Overture." I was playing more wrong notes than right ones. Our band director, Mr. Clint Walker, was fresh from a four-year tour with the U.S. Navy. His military experience, his stern personality, and his impressive physique combined to produce a formidable figure on the podium. I remember one day when he threw his baton at Gerald Pickens, the bass horn player. The baton missed Gerald and disappeared down the bell of the bass horn. Today was my day.

Following a particularly long sequence of wrong notes from me, Clint Walker stopped the band in mid-phrase. He did not throw the baton at me, choosing instead a more corrective weapon. He suggested that I hang a black crepe over my head because it was apparent to him that I was dead from the neck up. These were harsh words for a tender sixth-grader and, at the time, did nothing for my dignity. But the lesson was plain enough. I had not been practicing my instrument. He knew it. I knew it. I needed a prod. Was that an act of compassion. I think so.

There is more. Three years later, my Dad died and family finances were tight. I would not be able to pay my way to the three-week summer music camp that I had been attending for the past three years. One day as I was wandering down the main street of my hometown of Millington, Tennessee, guess who picked me up off the street? Yes, sir, that mean band director, Clint Walker. He told me to show up when the bus left for camp, and he would find a way for me to get a work scholarship to camp. Clint Walker loved me in his own gruff way. He expected the best that I could give. He would not let me cheat myself. He intervened in my life at an opportune moment with an act of caring, which has propelled me through a lot of fine living, at no cost to any organization that I can see.

In my career, I have profited from several mentors of moral knowledge and moral courage. They struggled to know what was right, to do what was right. Their investment in my life was at no expense to their organizations. Their expectations, their correction, their counsel, their encouragement — these were acts of compassion that strengthened my life. These were people different in personality, education, career, and position; but they all possessed a common devotion to those principles that mark the leader of integrity:

Curiosity. These were leaders in a community of learning. They modeled in their own lives what they expected in colleagues and students — a sustaining curiosity, an intense intellectual drive, an excitement and hunger for learning expressed in both reflection and action.

Candor. These were leaders who spoke the truth — with sensitivity when that was needed and with more force when that was appropriate. They asked for the truth, valued dissent, and were willing to endure the discomfort often carried by the truth. They were willing to test their decisions and values in the public forum, to open their principles and actions to public scrutiny.

Courtesy. These were leaders who treated each person within the circle of their influence with dignity. From professor to groundskeeper, from governor to student – all warranted their respect. They understood the reciprocity principle found in almost every great religious literature: Do unto others as you would have them do unto you. They resisted arrogance because arrogance offends a person's dignity.

Courage. These were leaders willing to risk and to dare, to stand in isolation, to test the correctness of an act against standards other than popularity, to try and to fail, to confront wrongdoing, to communicate directly and forthrightly whether the news was pleasurable or painful, and to accept the mistakes of self and others and learn from them.

Compassion. These were leaders who, though different in personality, showed compassion. They possessed the true mark of leadership integrity: they created hope and inspiration in others by investing colleagues with trust and high expectations, by opening opportunity for development.

Curiosity, Candor, Courtesy, Courage, Compassion – cynics will say that these are just empty words. The leaders I have just described taught me the meaning and depth of these simple but powerful words. Each day teachers and administrators continue to invest these words with meaning in education institutions all over this country.

These are leaders who do not shrink from their moral duty because of personality or performance imperfections. Those who have struggled and stumbled, fought and fallen, those who have risen to their feet and their faith will do so with a greater compassion than those small spirits whose virtue is narrow and brittle, never having been tested in the crucible of decision and action.

These are leaders who retreat not into the womb of ethical neutrality and irresponsibility when moral dilemma and complexity stress their minds and spirits. When honor, justice, and compassion still call but their guide is uncertain, here are men and women willing to reveal their humanity in its ultimate hour, struggling to know and to do what is right, furnishing those who follow with an intimate glimpse into the journey as well as the arrival of leadership. To those who invest the finest and highest values with meaning in their lives, to the leadership mentors in my life, and to thousands of others in our schools and universities – I salute you.

Duplicity is an enemy of leadership.

References

Alinsky, Saul D. *Rules for Radicals*. New York: Random House, 1971. Quotes from Vintage Books Edition, 1972.

Bennett, William J. "Getting Ethics." *Commentary* 70 (December 1980):62-65.

Bok, Sissela. *Lying*. New York: Random House, 1978. Quotes from Vintage Books Edition, 1979.

Buckley, William. "A Communist at Harvard." *Shreveport Times*, 8 August 1984, p. 5B.

Callahan, Daniel, and Bok, Sissela. "The Role of Applied Ethics in Learning." *Change* 7 (September 1979): 23-27.

Callahan, Daniel, and Bok, Sissela, eds. *Ethics Teaching in Higher Education*. New York: Plenum Press, 1980.

Carnegie Council on Policy Studies in Higher Education. *Fair Practices in Higher Education: Rights and Responsibilities of Students and Their Colleges in a Period of Intensified Competition for Enrollments*. San Francisco: Jossey-Bass, 1979.

"Conversation with Derek Bok: Students Need to Grapple with Significant Ethical Problems." *U.S. News and World Report*, 21 February 1983, p. 83.

Cush, Matthew. "Recent Buckley Column Presents Unsound Argument." *Shreveport Times*, 19 August 1984, Letters to the Editor, p. 9B.

Dill, David. "Introduction, Ethics and the Academic Profession." *Journal of Higher Education* 53 (May/June 1982): 243-52.

Enarson, Harold L. "The Ethical Imperative of the College Presidency." *Educational Record* 65 (Spring 1984): 24-26.

Rokeach, Milton. *The Nature of Human Values*. New York: Free Press, 1973.

Stein, Ronald H., et al., eds. *Professional Ethics in University Administration: New Directions for Higher Education*. San Francisco: Jossey-Bass, 1981.

The Teaching of Ethics in Higher Education: A Report by the Hasting Center. Hastings-on-Hudson, N.Y.: Institute of Society, Ethics and the Life Sciences, 1980.

Thompson, Victor A. *Without Sympathy or Enthusiasm: The Problem of Administrative Compassion*. University: University of Alabama Press, 1975.

Tuchman, Barbara. "The Missing Element: Moral Courage." In *In Search of Leaders*, edited by G. Kerry Smith et al. Washington, D.C.: American Association for Higher Education, 1967.

Walker, Donald. "The President as Ethical Leader of the Campus." In *Professional Ethics in University Administration*, edited by Ronald H. Stein et al. San Francisco: Jossey-Bass, 1981.

West, Morris L. *Daughter of Silence*. New York: William Morrow and Company, 1961.

Winterbotham, F. W. *The Ultra Secret*. New York: Harper & Row, 1974.